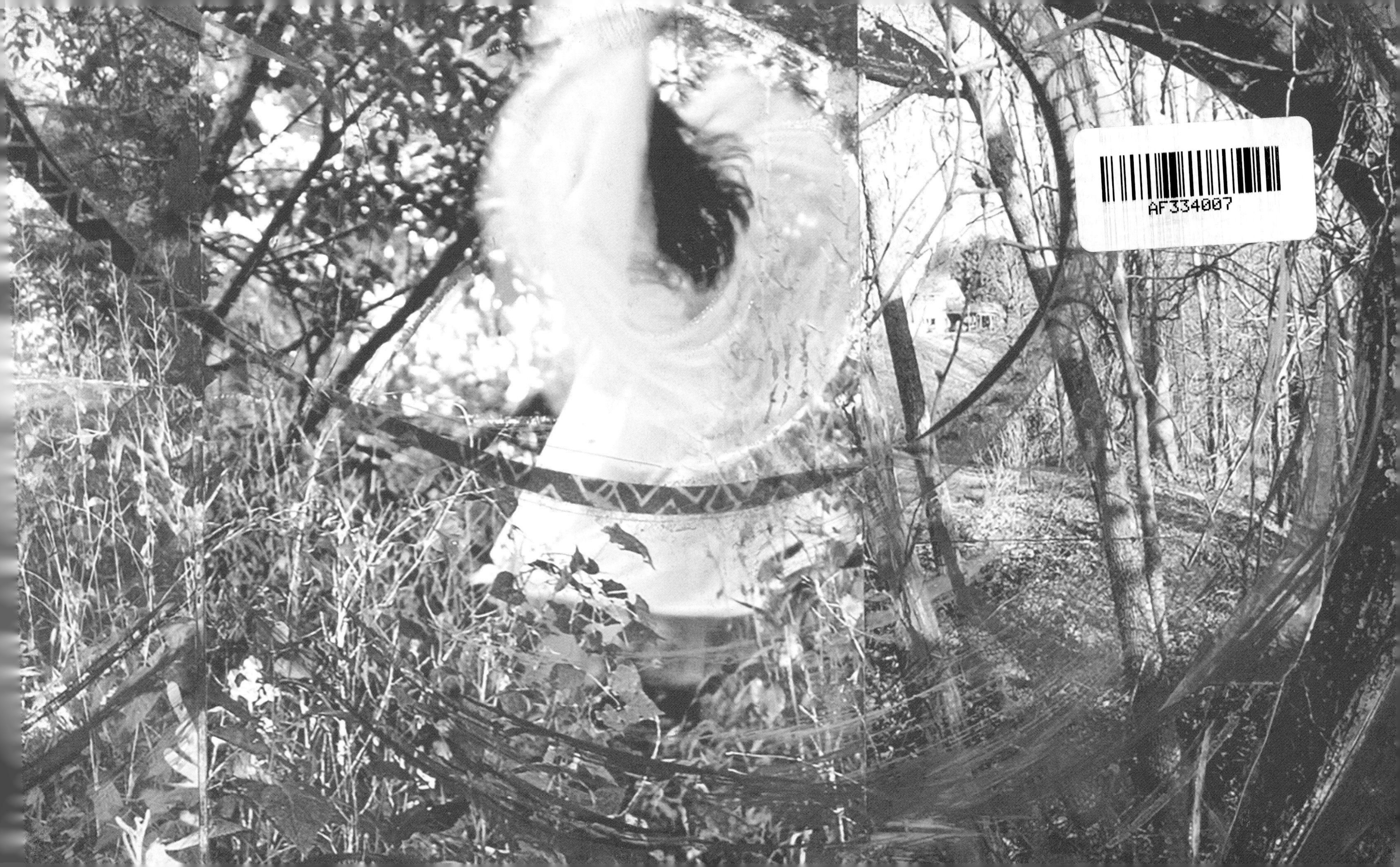
AF334007

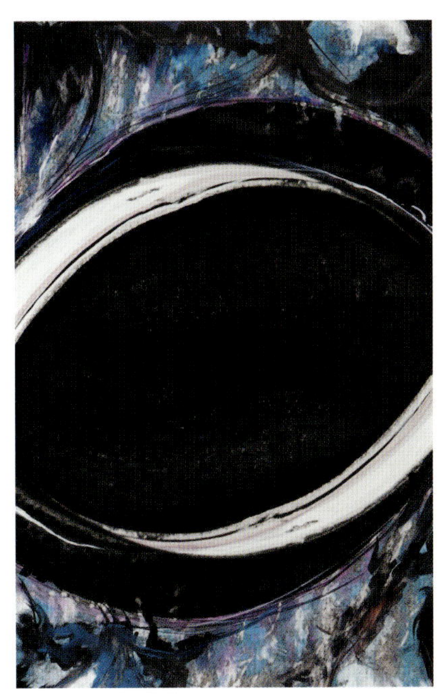 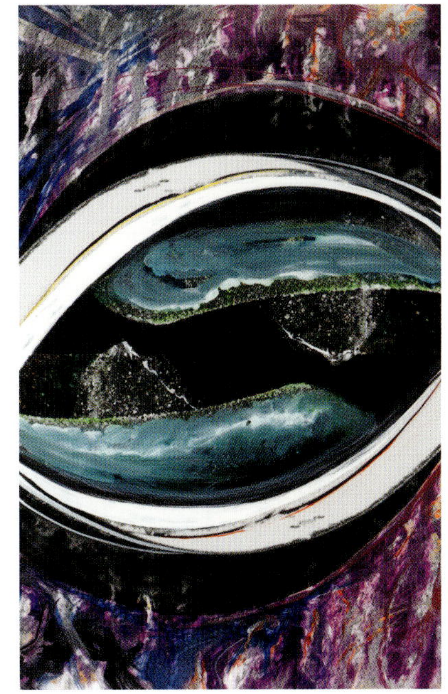 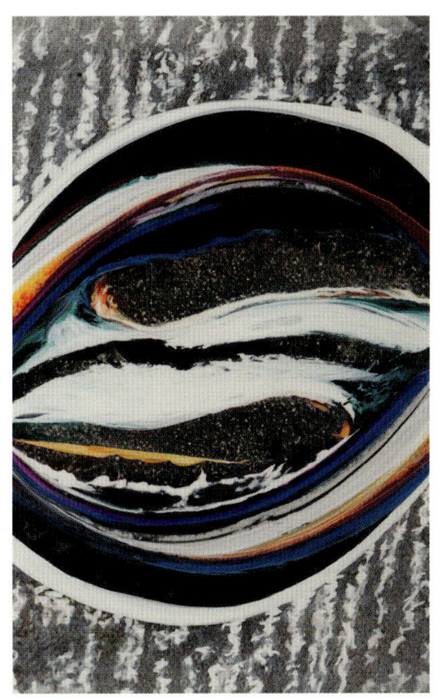

REVELATION PROJECT

MARILYN HICKEY   ART BY CYNTHIA STANCHAK

THE REVELATION PROJECT

Marilyn Hickey Ministries | P.O. Box 6598 | Englewood, CO 80155
www.marilynandsarah.org

Cynthia Stanchak | stanchakart.com | cynthia@stanchakart.com

Photographs of finished artwork and photographs of the artist by Becky Thurner Photography.

ISBN: 978-1-62911-777-5
Printed in the United States of America
© 2016 by Marilyn Hickey Ministries and Cynthia Stanchak

Whitaker House | 1030 Hunt Valley Circle | New Kensington, PA 15068
www.whitakerhouse.com

Library of Congress Cataloging-in-Publication Data

Names: Hickey, Marilyn, author. | Stanchak, Cynthia, 1957- illustrator.
Title: The Revelation project / Cynthia Stanchak and Marilyn Hickey.
Description: New Kensington, PA : Whitaker House, 2016.
Identifiers: LCCN 2016028712 | ISBN 9781629117775 (hardcover : alk. paper)
Subjects: LCSH: Bible. Revelation–Miscellanea. | Bible.
  Revelation–Illustrations.
Classification: LCC BS2825.55 .H53 2016 | DDC 228/.077–dc23 LC record available at
https://lccn.loc.gov/2016028712

1 2 3 4 5 6 7 8 9 10 ⅏ 23 22 21 20 19 18 17 16

CONTENTS

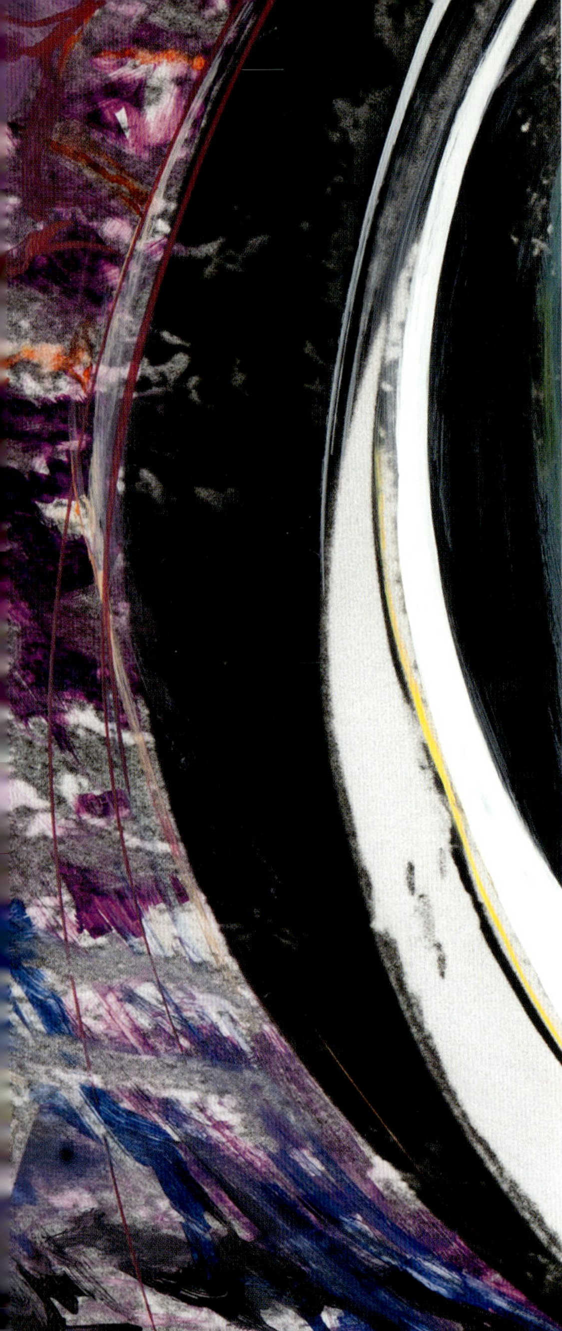

REVELATION

The book of Revelation has great purpose and great power. And yet, so many people don't read it. They feel that it is too difficult to interpret, that it scrambles their brain, that it is confusing—all of which is very understandable.

My passion and my goal in this book is to show the *simplicity* of the truth of Revelation in Jesus Christ. It is called the *Revelation of Jesus Christ*. That is exactly what it is. It is Jesus Christ for us to read and to experience. In Revelation we find God's wonderful love plan through Jesus Christ, revealing to us that we do not have to fear end-time events because we have a Redeemer who has purchased us with His blood. And His blood, His sacrifice, is our hope.

The book of Revelation is not a series of disconnected prophecies: it is a structured plan of love. This plan will encourage your heart toward belief and inspire others to believe as well. It is simply a *must* for you: experience this book of the plan of love! Finish its pages, and its purpose will find its finishing in your life. It provides an encouraging perspective both on the end-times and on current events.

I have a great desire to unscramble this much-debated book of the Bible and make it a *personal* Revelation of Jesus Christ to everyone!

Marilyn Hickey

PROJECT

My intention with this project was to reflect the peace and hope that I felt as I meditated on the book of Revelation.

In the artwork throughout this book, you will notice repetitive circular shapes beginning with a tilted axis and progressing into a parallel axis. These represent Christ's detailed plan to transform a fallen world. At first, it's seemingly spinning out of control, but as the book progresses, the depicted chaos is put back in order.

Not far into working on the project, it became imperative that I use my pile of scrap metal, vintage objects, and archival photographs to create art that portrays God's ultimate recycling plan of renewing the earth and all that He created. One of my favorite passages is Revelation 20:4, which tells us that all believers will join Him in restoring all things for one thousand years.

As I read about God's loving plan of redemption unfolding in the last few chapters of Revelation, I found myself overwhelmed by the depth of His love for all creation. This is when I painted the last two pieces: *Archol* and *The 3 Dimensions of Man*. These show the marriage of the bride and groom, and the reality that man is made in God's image.

Cynthia Stanchak

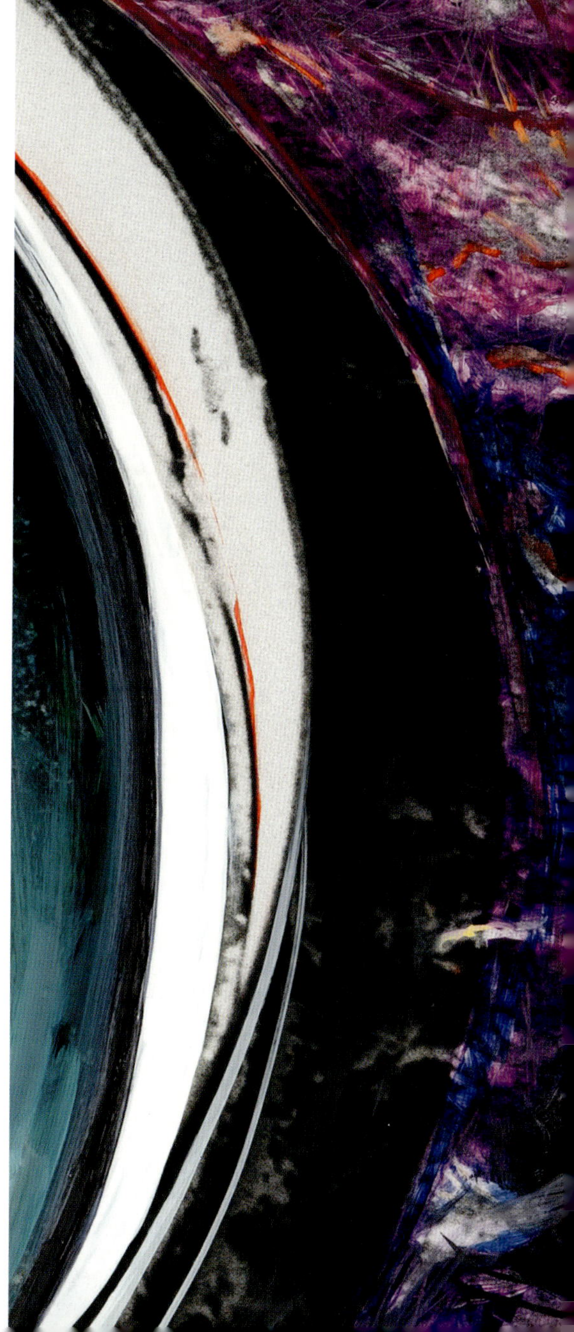

THE STRUCTURE OF REVELATION

Revelation can be conceptualized as a house with seven rooms.[1] In the first room is Christ, the Redeemer, and the Hero of the story. The second room is devoted to the churches–whom God uses in His process of redemption from Pentecost to the Rapture. Three doors open from the second room: one to heaven immediately following the Rapture (the third room), one to earth as the church experiences tribulation at the hand of the Antichrist (the fourth room), and one to Satan's church, which became an instrument in the persecution of the saints (fifth room). There is no doorway out of the fifth room, because everything there is destroyed.

The rooms of heaven and earth lead into the sixth room, the kingdom room, the climax of the ages. Creation then reaches the seventh and most glorious room: it is the very sanctuary of God. It is the Holy City that He will share with His saints forever.

When you walk through the seven rooms, as if walking through the seven rooms of a house, you see the plan and purpose of the end-times for yourself. Look up, because your redemption is drawing near! There are many things too wonderful for us to grasp, and yet, a picture can uncover the deepest mysteries in our minds. That is why it is so appropriate to ponder this book of the Bible through works of art.

The art of Cynthia Stanchak guides us through the textured, multi-layered, and symbolic nature of the book of Revelation by suggesting images to our hearts that interpret the words we see on the page and brings us one step closer to our King. Verses from Revelation are woven through this book, not for the purpose of definitive interpretation, but to keep God's Word close to our imaginations as we ponder the end-times.

As God pictures this house with seven rooms in your heart, remember that God loves us into eternity with an extravagant love.

1. The seven-room interpretation of the book of Revelation is taken from Arthur Bloomfield, *All Things New: A Study of Revelation*, Bethany Fellowship, 1959, reprinted 1963.

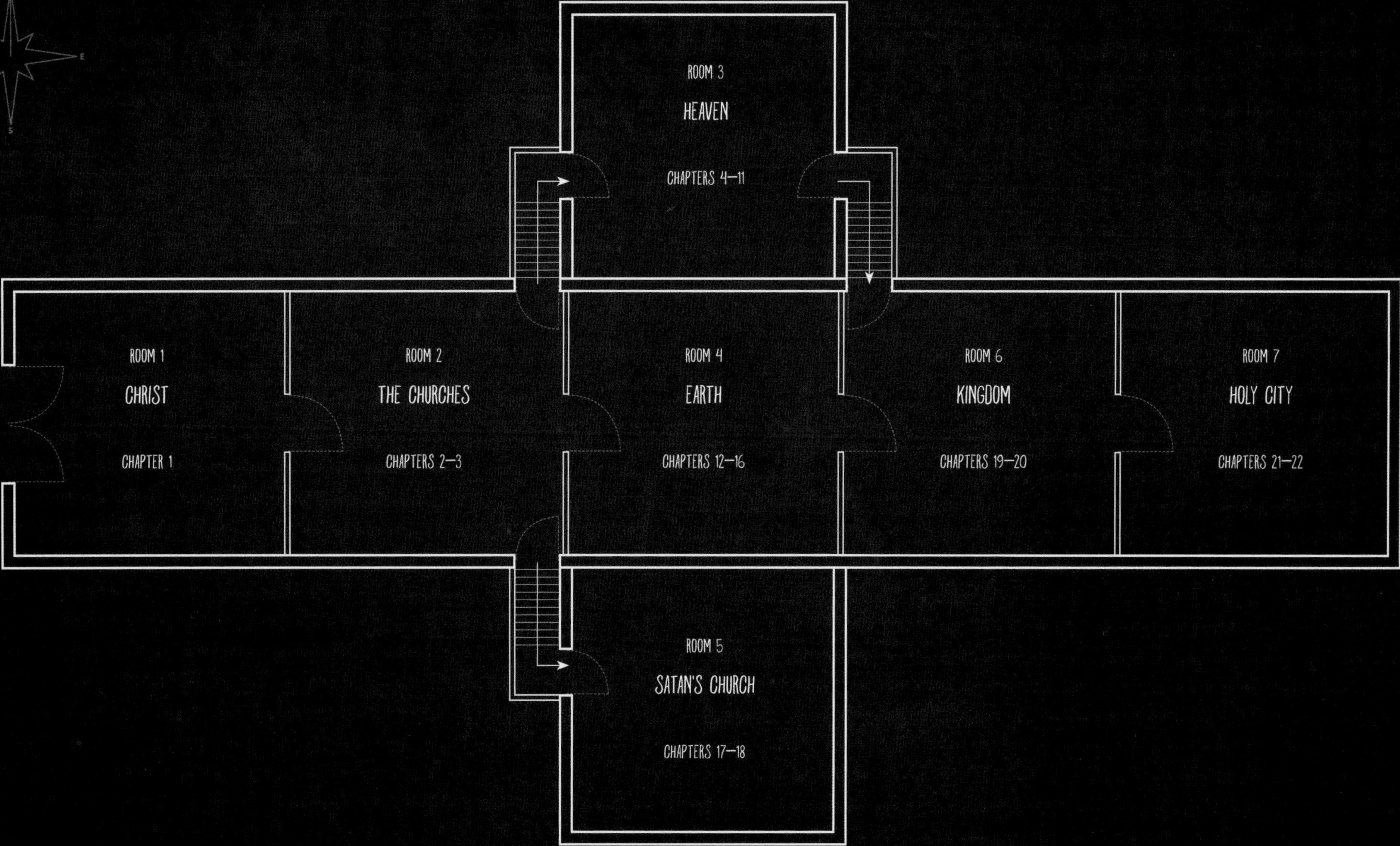

E
S
ROOM 3
HEAVEN
CHAPTERS 4–11
ROOM 1
CHRIST
CHAPTER 1
ROOM 2
THE CHURCHES
CHAPTERS 2–3
ROOM 4
EARTH
CHAPTERS 12–16
ROOM 6
KINGDOM
CHAPTERS 19–20
ROOM 7
HOLY CITY
CHAPTERS 21–22
ROOM 5
SATAN'S CHURCH
CHAPTERS 17–18

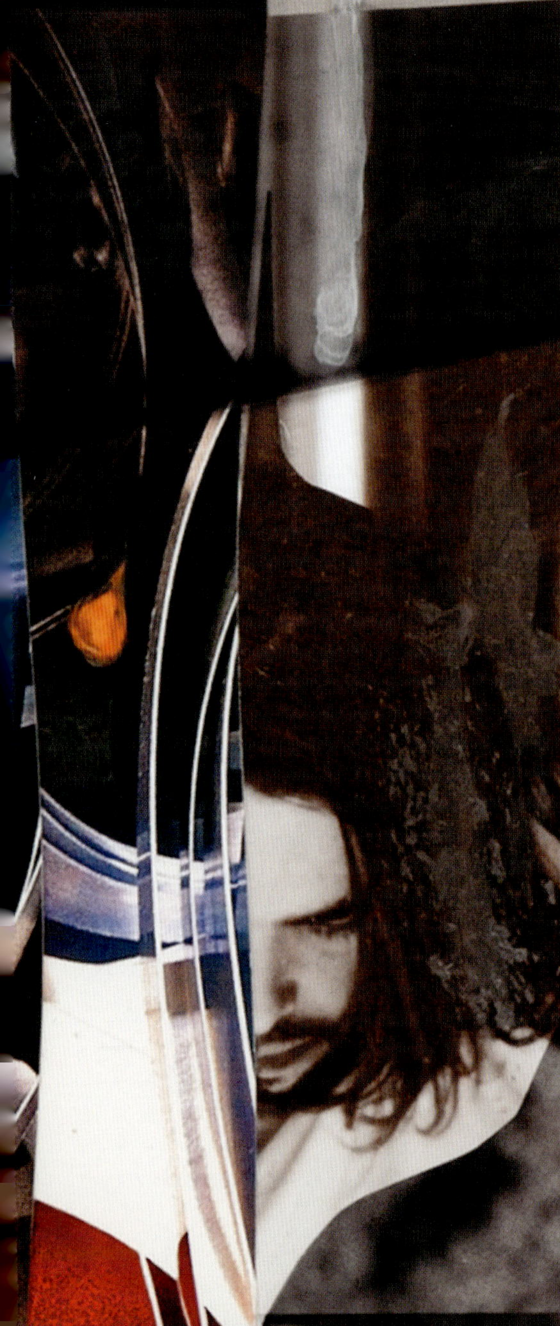

1

The Revelation of Jesus Christ, which God gave unto Him, to show to His servants things which must shortly come to pass; and He sent and signified it by His angel to His servant John: who bore record of the word of God, and of the testimony of Jesus Christ, and of all things that he saw. Blessed is he that reads, and they that hear the words of this prophecy, and keep those things which are written therein: for the time is at hand.

John to the seven churches which are in Asia: Grace be to you, and peace, from Him which is, and which was, and which is to come; and from the seven Spirits which are before His throne; and from Jesus Christ, who is the faithful witness, and the First Begotten of the dead, and the Prince of the kings of the earth. To Him that loved us, and washed us from our sins in His own blood, and has made us kings and priests to God and His Father; to Him be glory and dominion for ever and ever. Amen.

Behold, He comes with clouds; and every eye shall see Him, and they also which pierced Him: and all kindreds of the earth shall wail because of Him. Even so, Amen. I am Alpha and Omega, the beginning and the ending, says the Lord, which is, and which was, and which is to come, the Almighty.

I John, who also am your brother, and companion in tribulation, and in the kingdom and patience of Jesus Christ, was in the isle that is called Patmos, for the word of God, and for the testimony of Jesus Christ. I was in the Spirit on the Lord's day, and heard behind me a great voice, as of a trumpet, saying, I am Alpha and Omega, the first and the last: and, What you see, write in a book, and send it to the seven churches which are in Asia; unto Ephesus, and to Smyrna, and to Pergamos, and to Thyatira, and to Sardis, and to Philadelphia, and to Laodicea.

And I turned to see the voice that spoke with me. And being turned, I saw seven golden candlesticks; and in the midst of the seven candlesticks one like to the Son of man, clothed with a garment down to the foot, and girt about the breasts with a golden girdle. His head and His hairs were white like wool, as white as snow; and His eyes were as a flame of fire; and His feet like to fine brass, as if they burned in a furnace; and His voice as the sound of many waters. And He had in His right hand seven stars: and out of His mouth went a sharp two edged sword: and His countenance was as the sun shines in His strength.

And when I saw Him, I fell at His feet as dead. And He laid His right hand upon me, saying to me, Fear not; I am the First and the Last: I am He that lives, and was dead; and, behold, I am alive for evermore, Amen; and have the keys of hell and of death. Write the things which you have seen, and the things which are, and the things which shall be hereafter; the mystery of the seven stars which you saw in My right hand, and the seven golden candlesticks. The seven stars are the angels of the seven churches: and the seven candlesticks which you saw are the seven churches.

ROOM 1

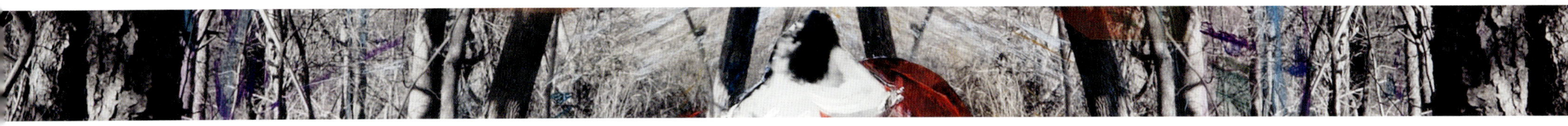

PICTURES OF THE RISEN CHRIST

This is a book about the end-times.

It is inspired by the hopelessness, the fire, the loss that we see all around us.

But it is a book of hope, of the total restoration to come, of the greatest love story ever lived.

*"Write the things which you have seen,
and the things which are and the things which shall be"* (Revelation 1:19).

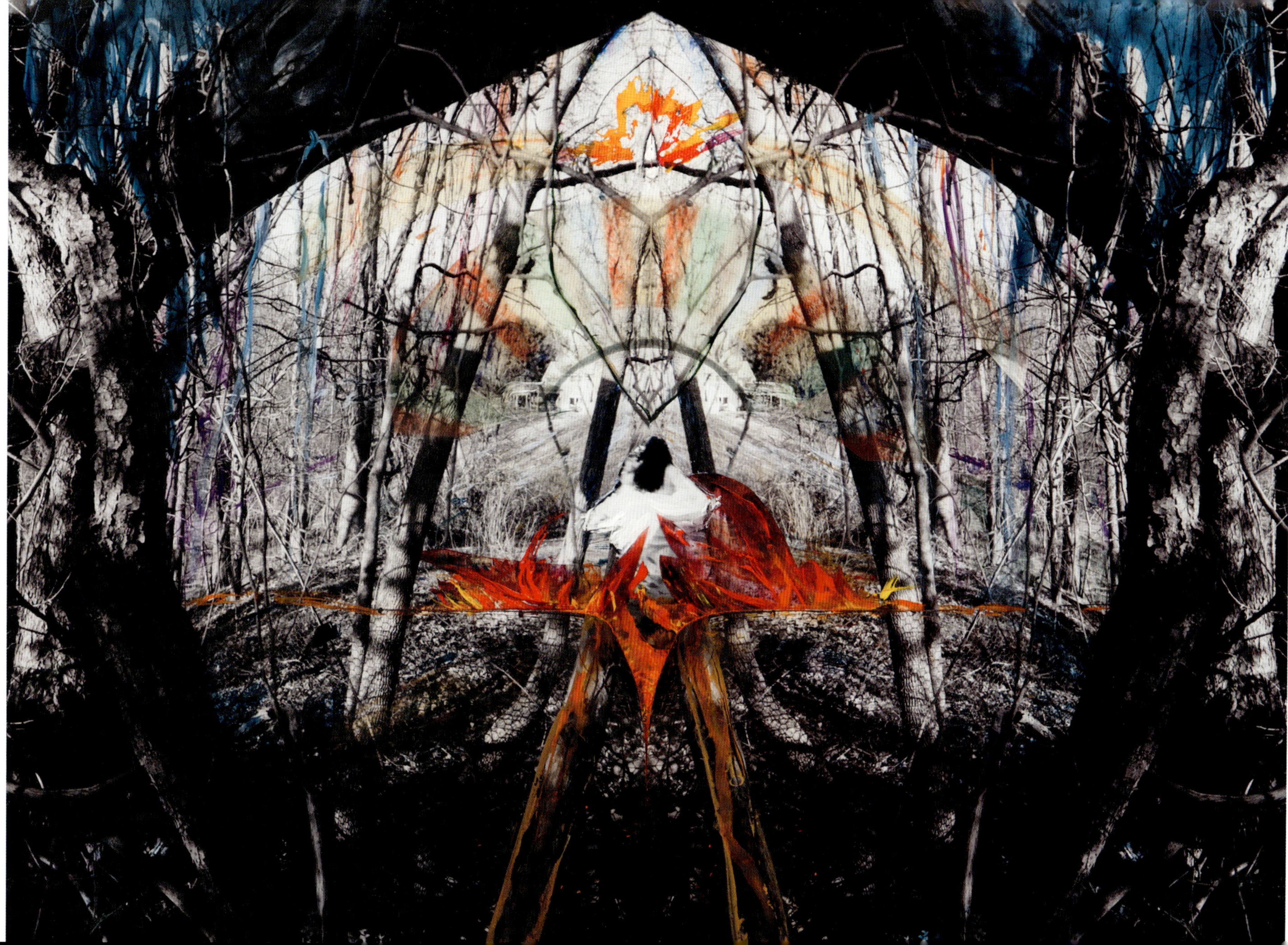

SPOTLESS

THE WORLD'S AXIS IN ITS FALLEN STATE INDICATES THE PRESENT CONDITION OF THE WORLD.

Look at the brightness of His love! Experience His love.

We see Jesus in His glorified body, standing before His churches.
But the first room not only reveals Jesus to the churches, it also reveals the glorified
Jesus that is in your present—in your today. He alone is spotless in our fallen world.

"To Him that loved us, and washed us from our sins in His own blood" (Revelation 1:5).

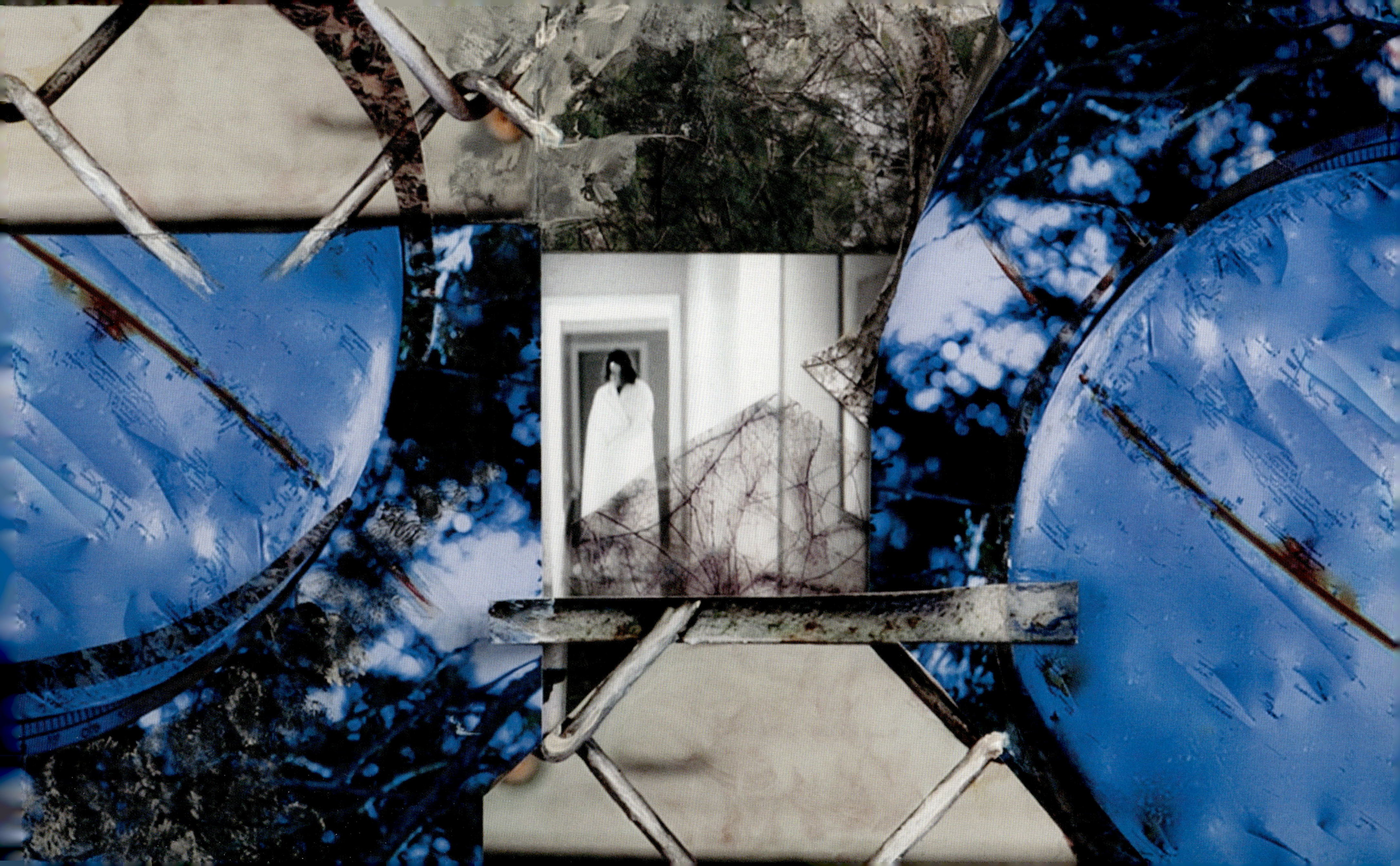

The whole world, its past, present, and future, is in His hands.

"I am the Alpha and the Omega, the first and the last" (Revelation 1:11).

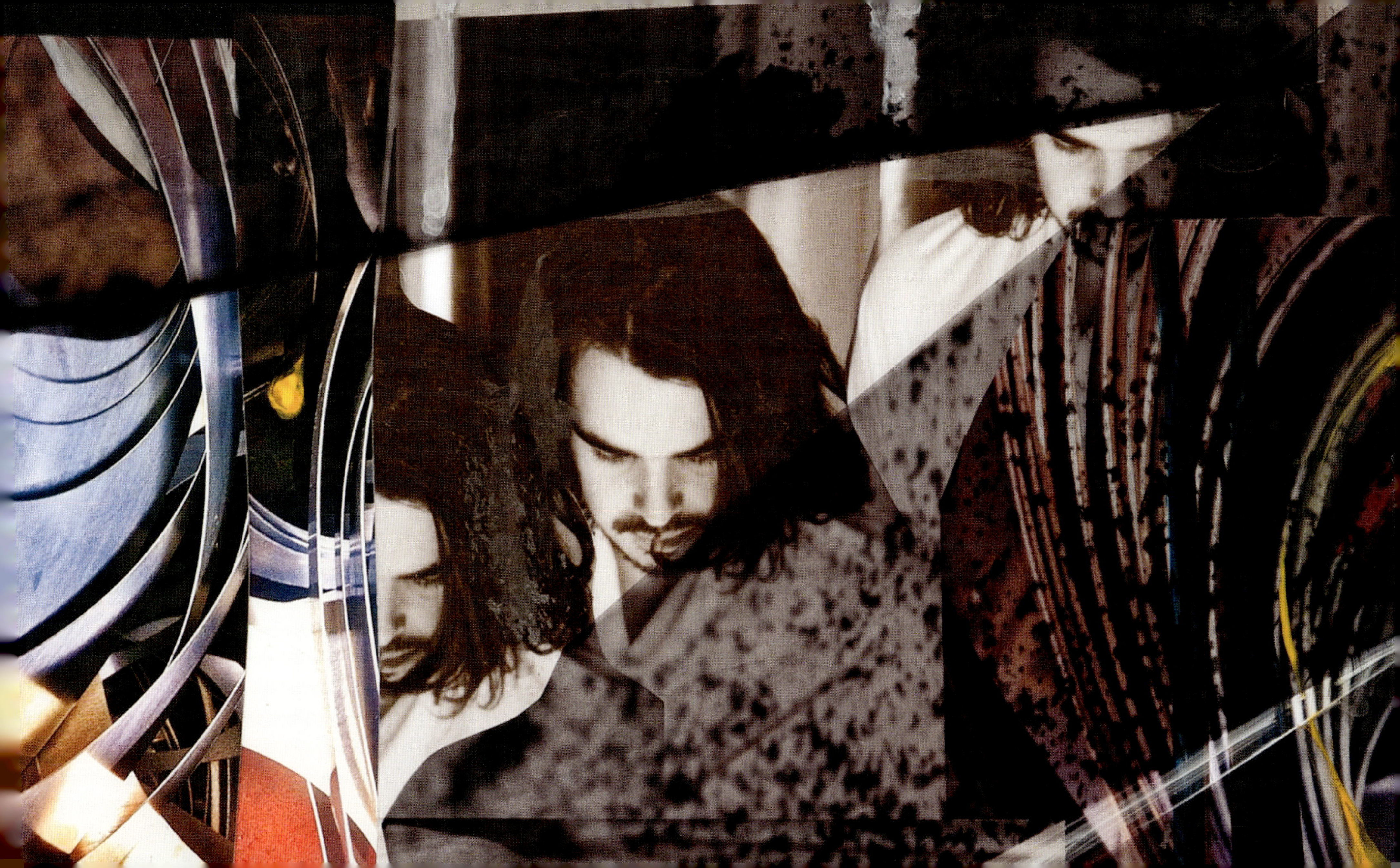

PERFECT STATE

A GLIMPSE OF THE WORLD'S AXIS IS HERE RESTORED TO ITS ORIGINAL POSITION.

The Redeemer's heart will always, and always promises to,
restore creation to its perfect state.

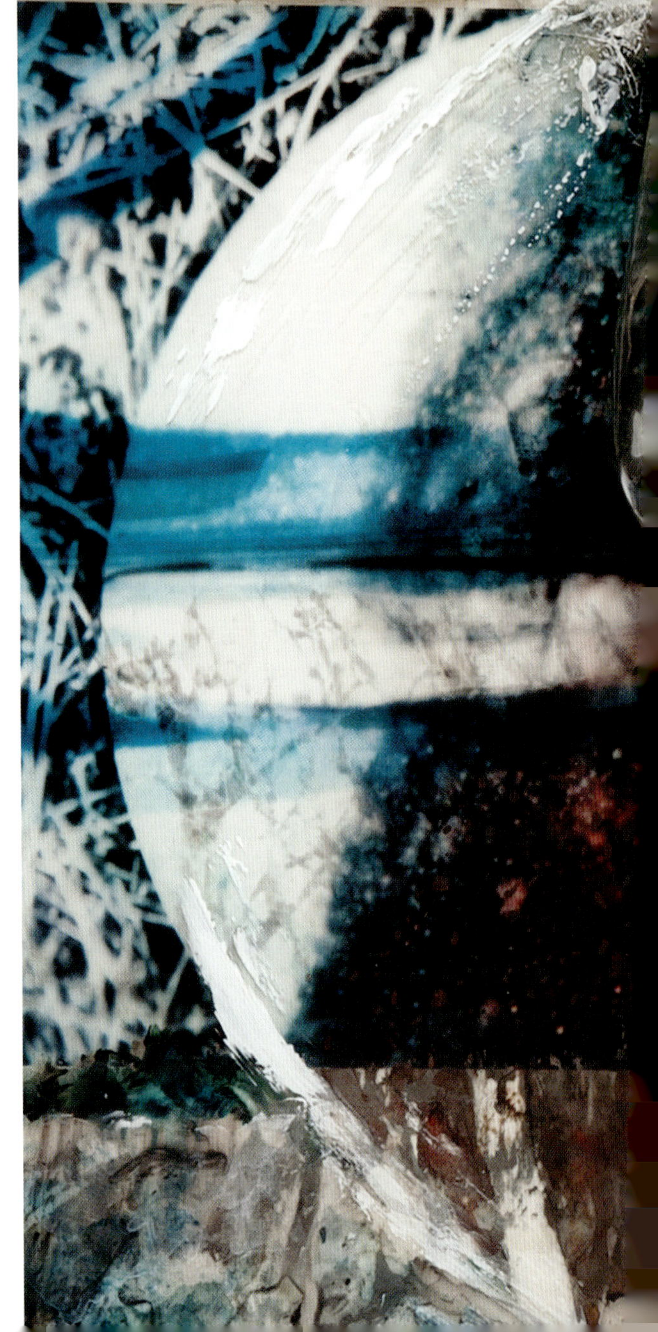

*"Behold, He comes with clouds; and every eye shall see Him,
and they also which pierced Him"* (Revelation 1:7).

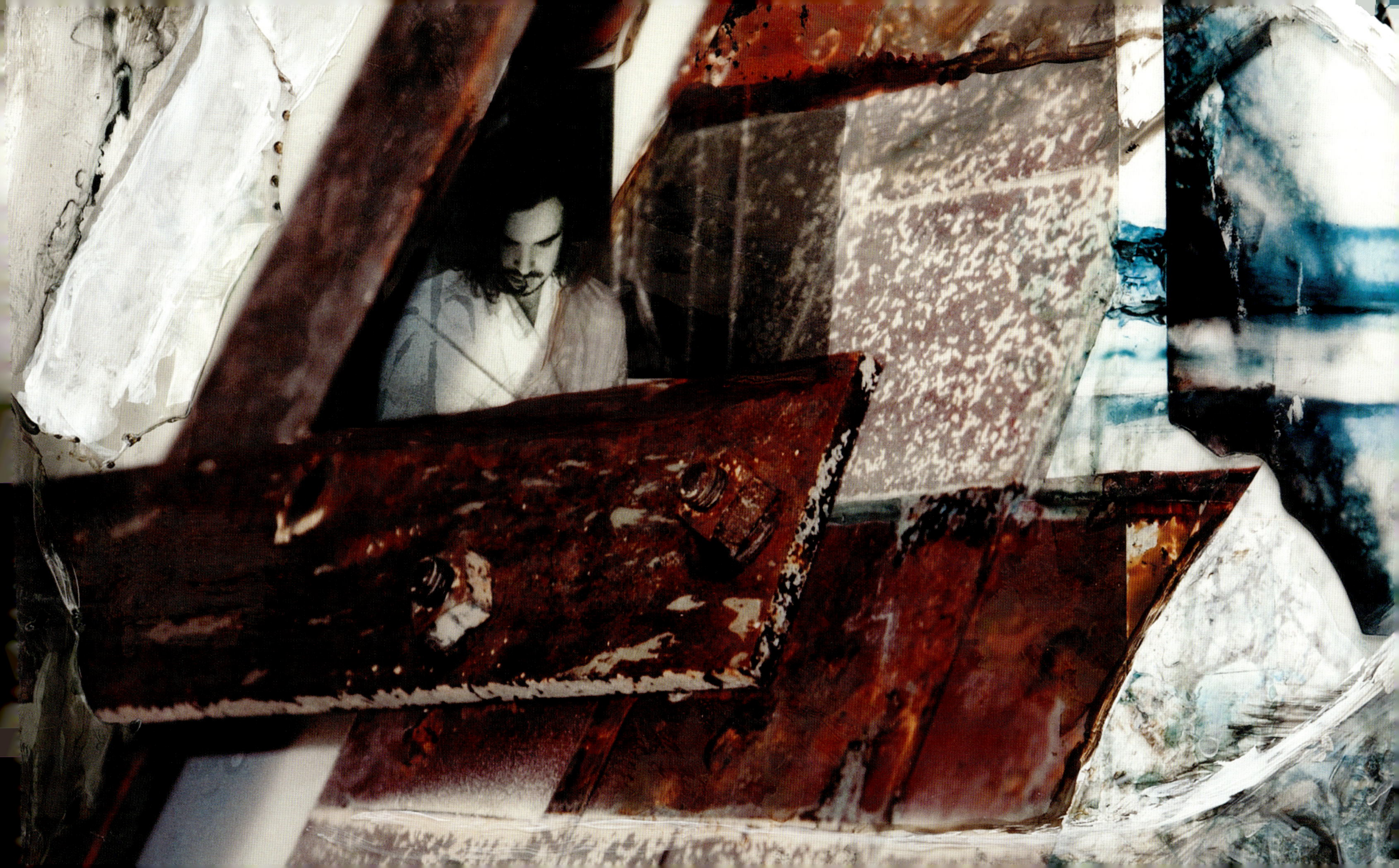

2–3

To the angel of the church of Ephesus write; These things says He that holds the seven stars in His right hand, who walks in the midst of the seven golden candlesticks; I know your works, and your labor, and your patience, and how you can not bear them which are evil: and you have tried them which say they are apostles, and are not, and have found them liars: and have borne, and have patience, and for My name's sake have labored, and have not fainted.

Nevertheless I have something against you, because you have left your first love. Remember therefore from where you art fallen, and repent, and do the first works; or else I will come to you quickly, and will remove your candlestick out of its place, except you repent. But this you have, that you hate the deeds of the Nicolaitanes, which I also hate.

He that has an ear, let him hear what the Spirit says to the churches; To him that overcomes will I give to eat of the tree of life, which is in the midst of the paradise of God.

And to the angel of the church in Smyrna write; These things says the First and the Last, which was dead, and is alive; I know your works, and tribulation, and poverty, (but you are rich) and I know the blasphemy of them which say they are Jews, and are not, but are the synagogue of Satan. Fear none of those things which you shall suffer: behold, the devil shall cast some of you into prison, that you may be tried; and you shall have tribulation ten days: be you faithful to death, and I will give you a crown of life.

He that has an ear, let him hear what the Spirit says to the churches; He that overcomes shall not be hurt of the second death.

And to the angel of the church in Pergamos write; These things says He which has the sharp sword with two edges; I know your works, and where you dwell, even where Satan's seat is: and you hold fast My name, and have not denied My faith, even in those days wherein Antipas was My faithful martyr, who was slain among you, where Satan dwell. But I have a few things against you, because you have there them that hold the doctrine of Balaam, who taught Balak to cast a stumbling block before the children of Israel, to eat things sacrificed to idols, and to commit fornication. So have you also them that hold the doctrine of the Nicolaitanes, which thing I hate. Repent; or else I will come to you quickly, and will fight against them with the sword of My mouth.

He that has an ear, let him hear what the Spirit says to the churches; To him that overcomes will I give to eat of the hidden manna, and will give him a white stone, and in the stone a new name written, which no man knows saving he that receives it.

And to the angel of the church in Thyatira write; These things says the Son of God, who has His eyes like to a flame of fire, and His feet are like fine brass; I know your works, and charity, and service, and faith, and your patience, you're your works; and the last to be more than the first. Notwithstanding I have a few things against you, because you permit that woman Jezebel, which calls herself a prophetess, to teach and to seduce My servants to commit fornication, and to eat things sacrificed to idols. And I gave her space to repent of her fornication; and she repented not. Behold, I will cast her into a bed, and them that commit adultery with her into great tribulation, except they repent of their deeds. And I will kill her children with death; and all the churches shall know that I am He which searches the reins and hearts: and I will give to every one of you according to your works. But to you I say, and to the rest in Thyatira, as many as have not this doctrine,

and which have not known the depths of Satan, as they speak; I will put upon you no other burden. But that which you have already hold fast till I come. And he that overcomes, and keeps My works unto the end, to him will I give power over the nations: and he shall rule them with a rod of iron; as the vessels of a potter shall they be broken to shivers: even as I received of My Father. And I will give him the morning star.

He that has an ear, let him hear what the Spirit says to the churches.

And unto the angel of the church in Sardis write; These things says He that has the seven Spirits of God, and the seven stars; I know your works, that you have a name that you live, and are dead. Be watchful, and strengthen the things which remain, that are ready to die: for I have not found your works perfect before God. Remember therefore how you have received and heard, and hold fast, and repent. If therefore you shalt not watch, I will come on you as a thief, and you shall not know what hour I will come upon you. You have a few names even in Sardis which have not defiled their garments; and they shall walk with Me in white: for they are worthy. He that overcomes, the same shall be clothed in white raiment; and I will not blot out his name out of the book of life, but I will confess his name before My Father, and before His angels. He that has an ear, let him hear what the Spirit says to the churches.

And to the angel of the church in Philadelphia write; These things says He that is holy, He that is true, He that has the key of David, He that opens, and no man shuts; and shuts, and no man opens; I know your works: behold, I have set before you an open door, and no man can shut it: for you have a little strength, and have kept My word, and have not denied My name. Behold, I will make them of the synagogue of Satan, which say they are Jews, and are not, but do lie; behold, I will make them to come

and worship before your feet, and to know that I have loved you. Because you have kept the word of My patience, I also will keep you from the hour of temptation, which shall come upon all the world, to try them that dwell upon the earth. Behold, I come quickly: hold that fast which you have, that no man take your crown. Him that overcomes will I make a pillar in the temple of My God, and he shall go no more out: and I will write upon him the name of My God, and the name of the city of My God, which is new Jerusalem, which comes down out of heaven from My God: and I will write upon him My new name.

He that has an ear, let him hear what the Spirit says unto the churches.

And to the angel of the church of the Laodiceans write; These things says the Amen, the faithful and true witness, the beginning of the creation of God; I know your works, that you are neither cold nor hot: I would you were cold or hot. So then because you are lukewarm, and neither cold nor hot, I will spew you out of My mouth. Because you say, I am rich, and increased with goods, and have need of nothing; and know not that you are wretched, and miserable, and poor, and blind, and naked: I counsel you to buy of Me gold tried in the fire, that you may be rich; and white raiment, that you may be clothed, and that the shame of your nakedness do not appear; and anoint your eyes with eye salve, that you may see. As many as I love, I rebuke and chasten: be zealous therefore, and repent. Behold, I stand at the door, and knock: if any man hear My voice, and open the door, I will come in to him, and will sup with him, and he with Me. To him that overcomes will I grant to sit with Me in My throne, even as I also overcame, and am set down with My Father in His throne.

He that has an ear, let him hear what the Spirit says to the churches.

ROOM 2

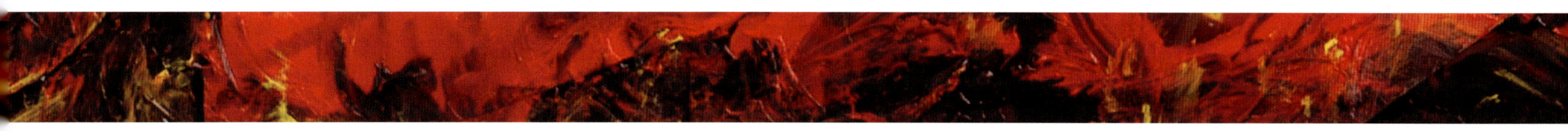

THE CHURCHES

CRIMSON SHROUD

THE FIGURE IN THE CENTER REPRESENTS THE SEVEN CHURCHES, SURROUNDED IN A
PROTECTIVE SHELL, AND HOLDING THE CRIMSON SHROUD.

The church pays a price to walk in victory.

"And [you] *have borne, and have patience, and for My name's sake have labored, and have not fainted"* (Revelation 2:3).

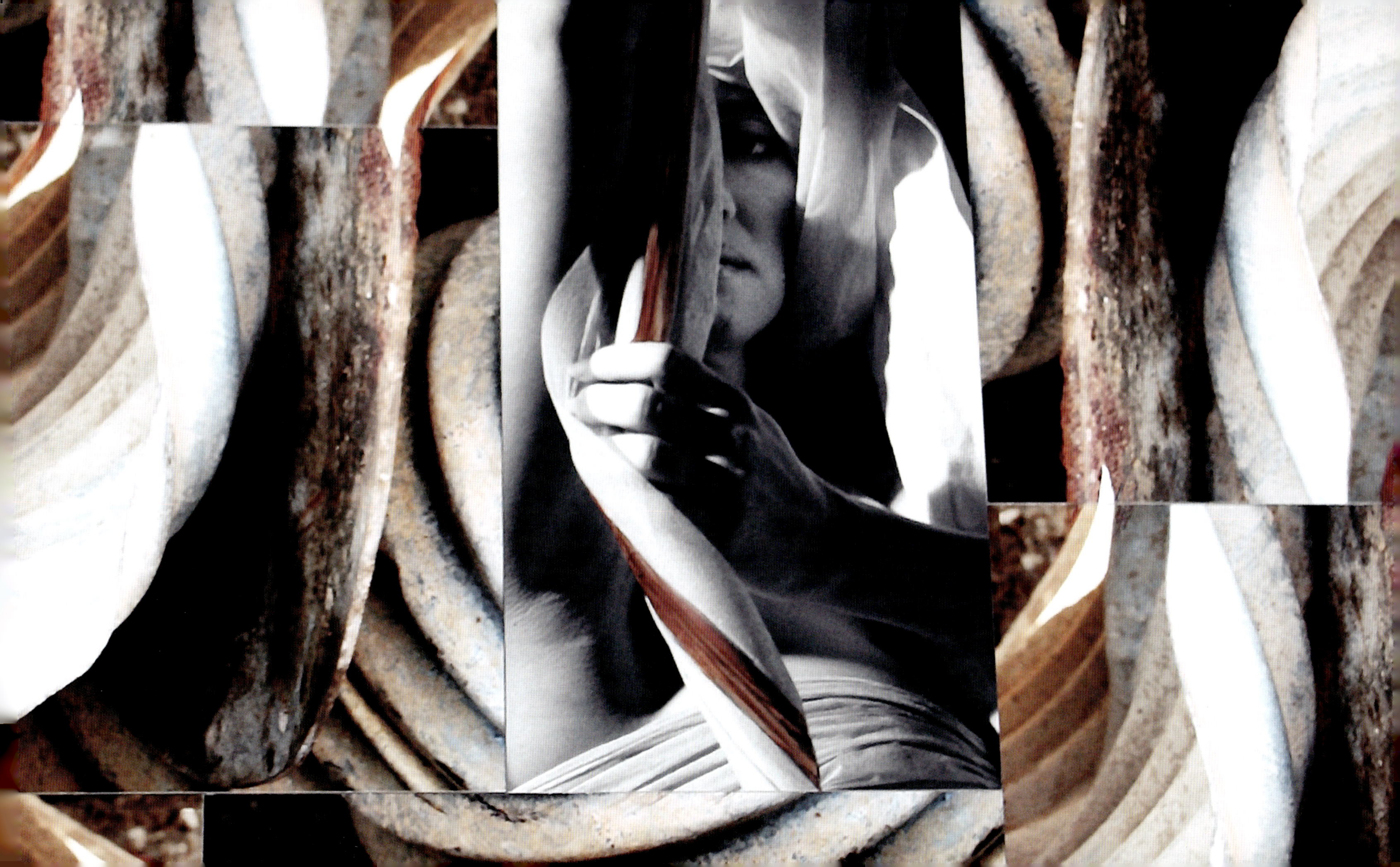

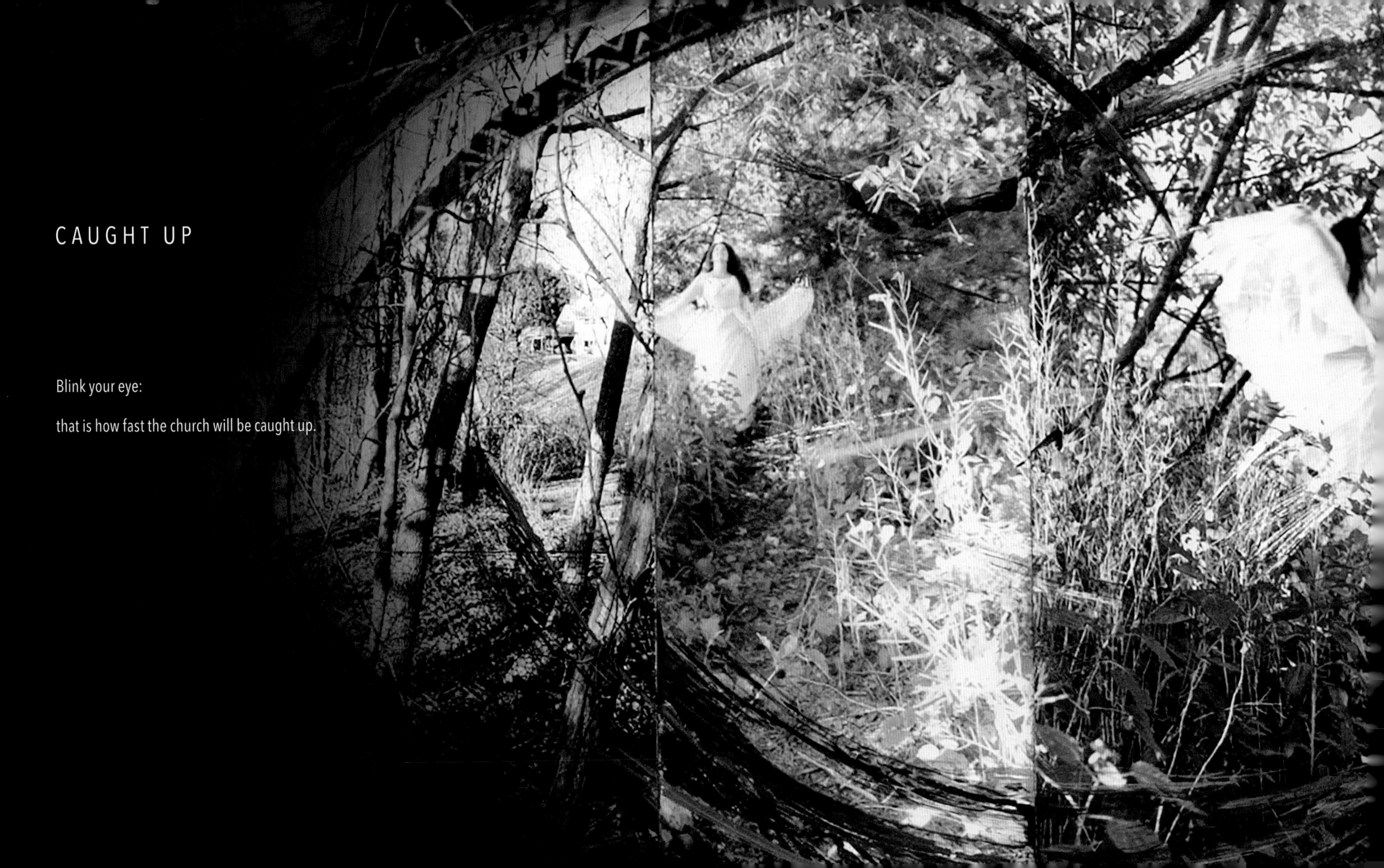
CAUGHT UP

Blink your eye:

that is how fast the church will be caught up.

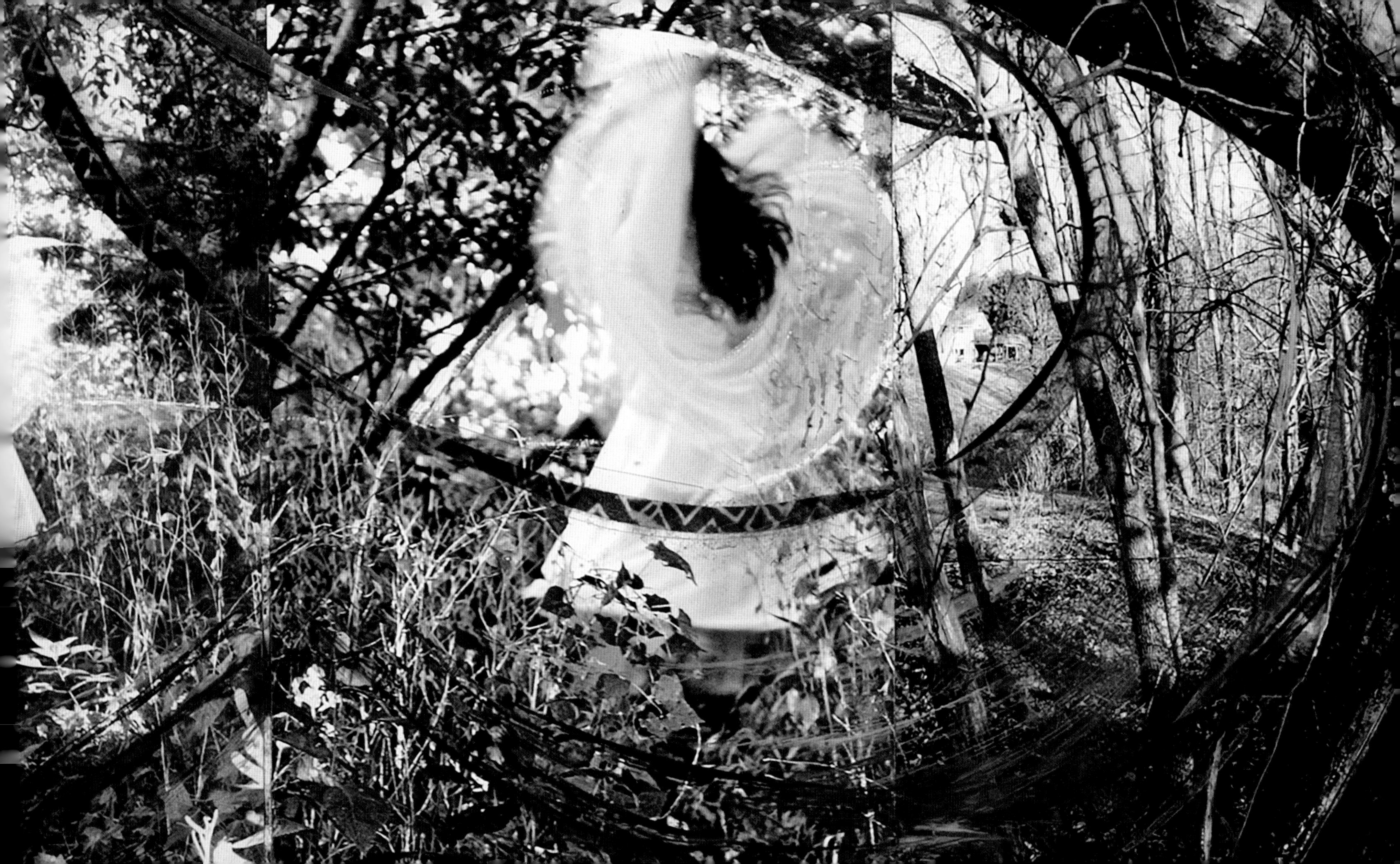

THE COMPROMISING CHURCH

AFTER LAYERING MULTIPLE PHOTOGRAPHS, I PULLED DOWN THE BOTTOM EDGES PRIOR
TO THE ADHESIVE DRYING TO FURTHER EXPOSE THE FACE. THE CHURCH PEEKS OUT FROM
BEHIND THE STEEL WALLS BUT DOES NOT FULLY COMMIT.

We see the church shaken.

"You have left your first love" (Revelation 2:4).

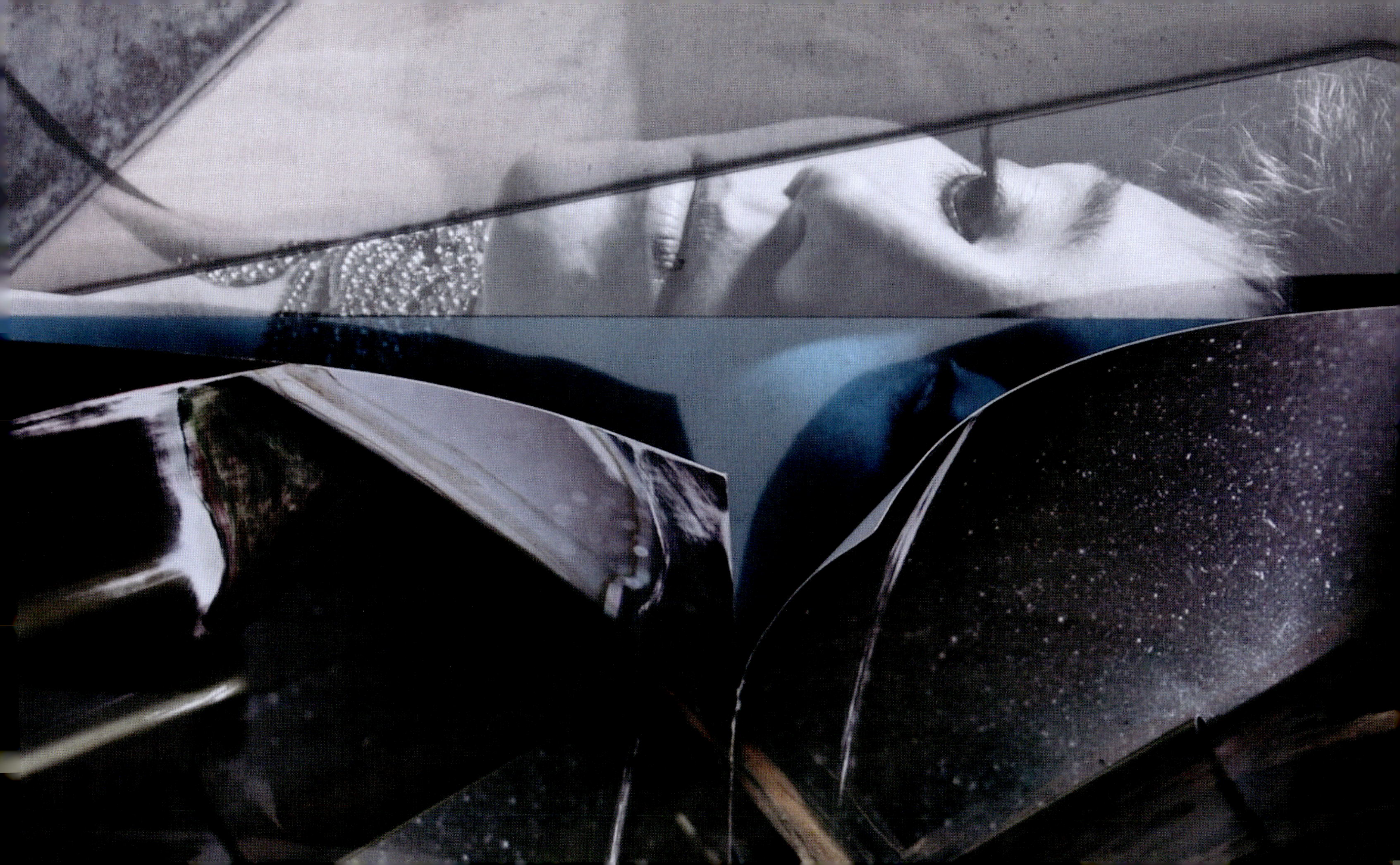

MONOFRACTION

We see the church settling for mediocracy.

"I know your works, that you are neither cold nor hot: I would you were cold or hot.
So then because you are lukewarm, and neither cold nor hot,
I will spew you out of My mouth" (Revelation 3:15-16).

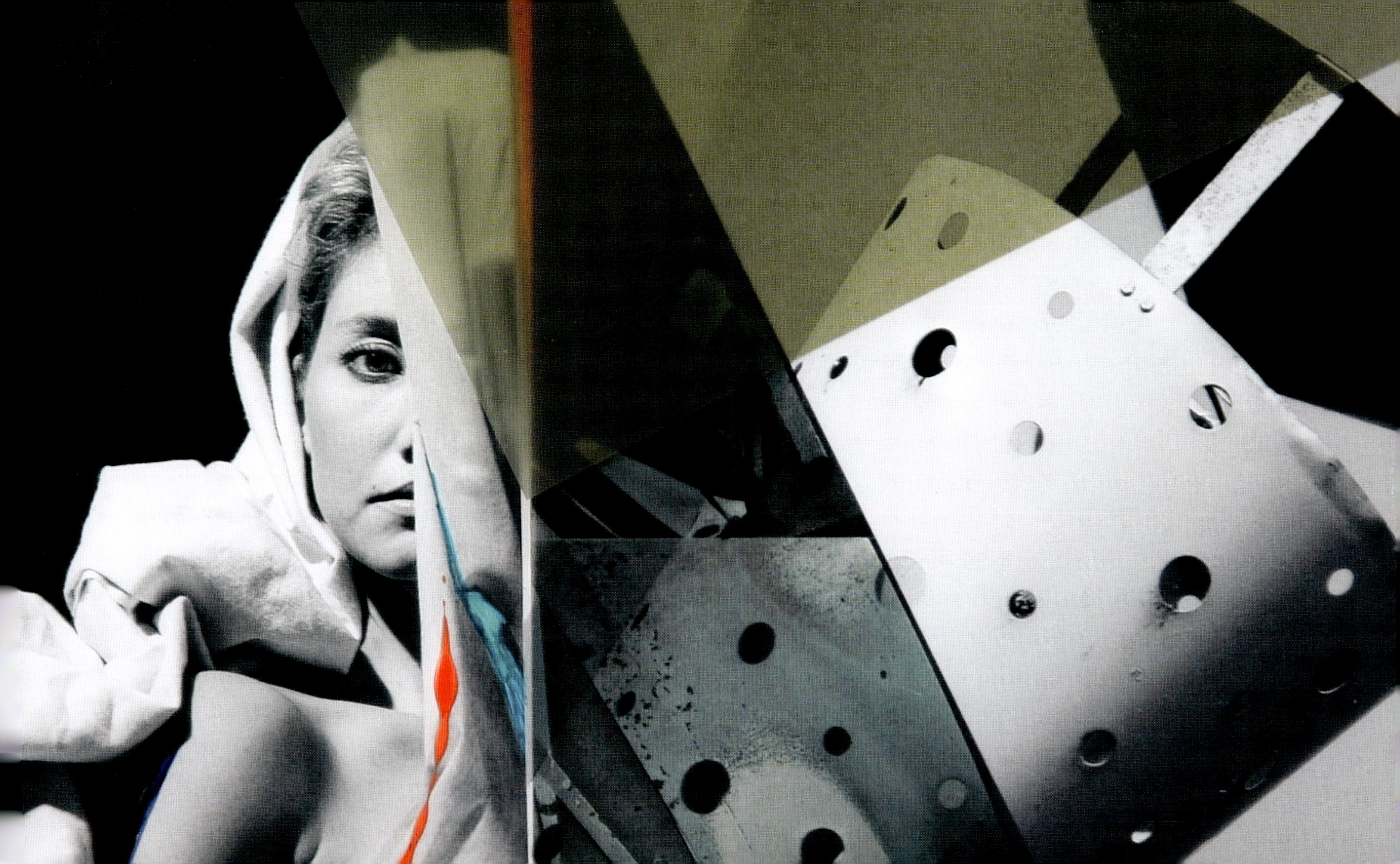

THE OVERCOMING CHURCH

THE FIERY EFFECT WAS ACHIEVED BY PHOTOGRAPHING A SMALL, THREE-DIMENSIONAL COMPOSITION MADE OF TOOTHPICKS THAT I PLACED INSIDE A PAPER BAG AND SHONE A LIGHT ON; I THEN ROLLED THE EDGES OF THE PRINTED IMAGE AND BURNT THEM.

We don't leave the earth as a negative church, but as a triumphant church.

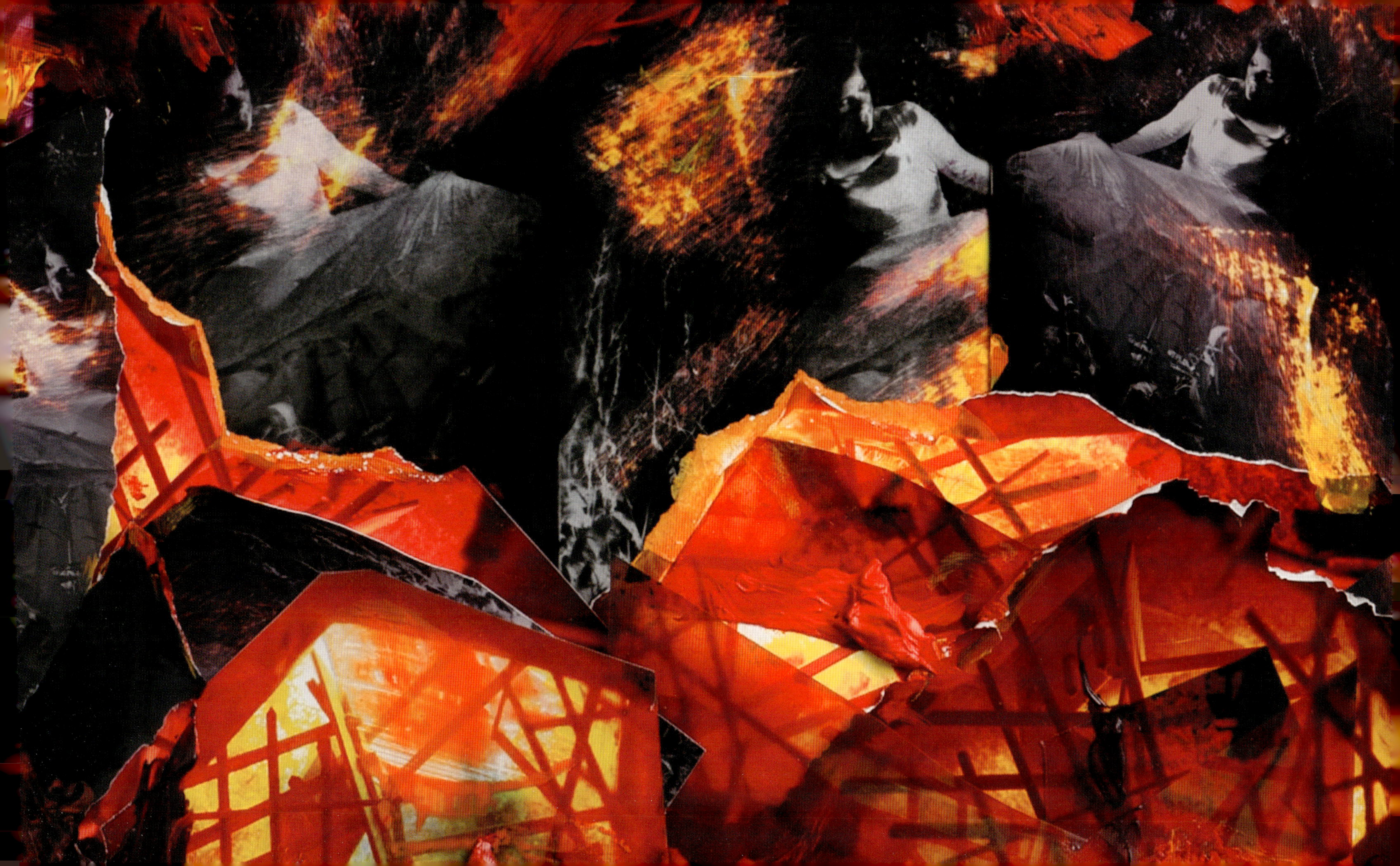

SHROUDED SALVATION

Does Jesus sometimes seem hidden to you?
Sometimes when the world closes in around us, we think, *Where is Jesus?*
But He is near; He clothes us in salvation.

"I counsel you to buy of me…white raiment, that you may be clothed"
(Revelation 3:18).

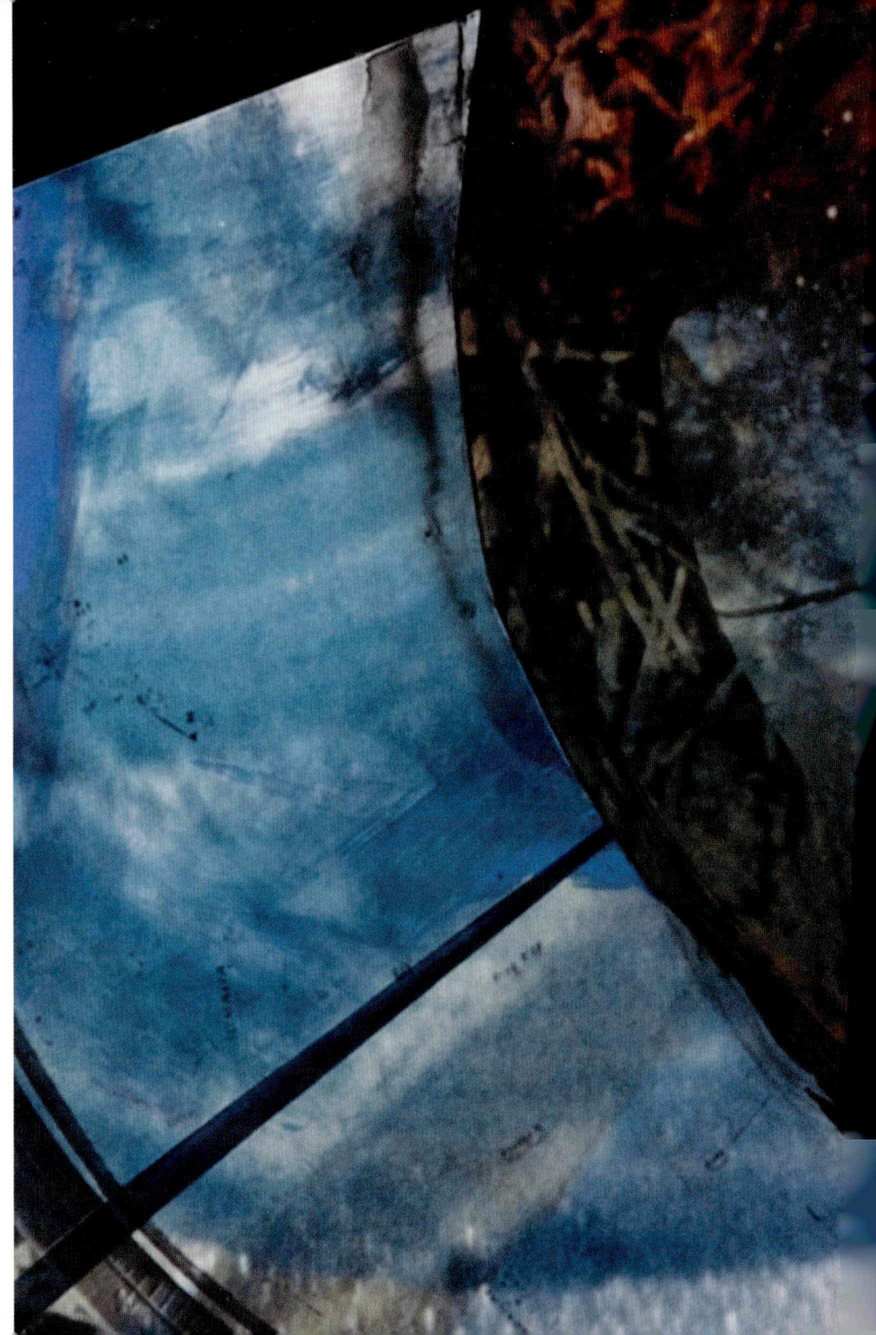

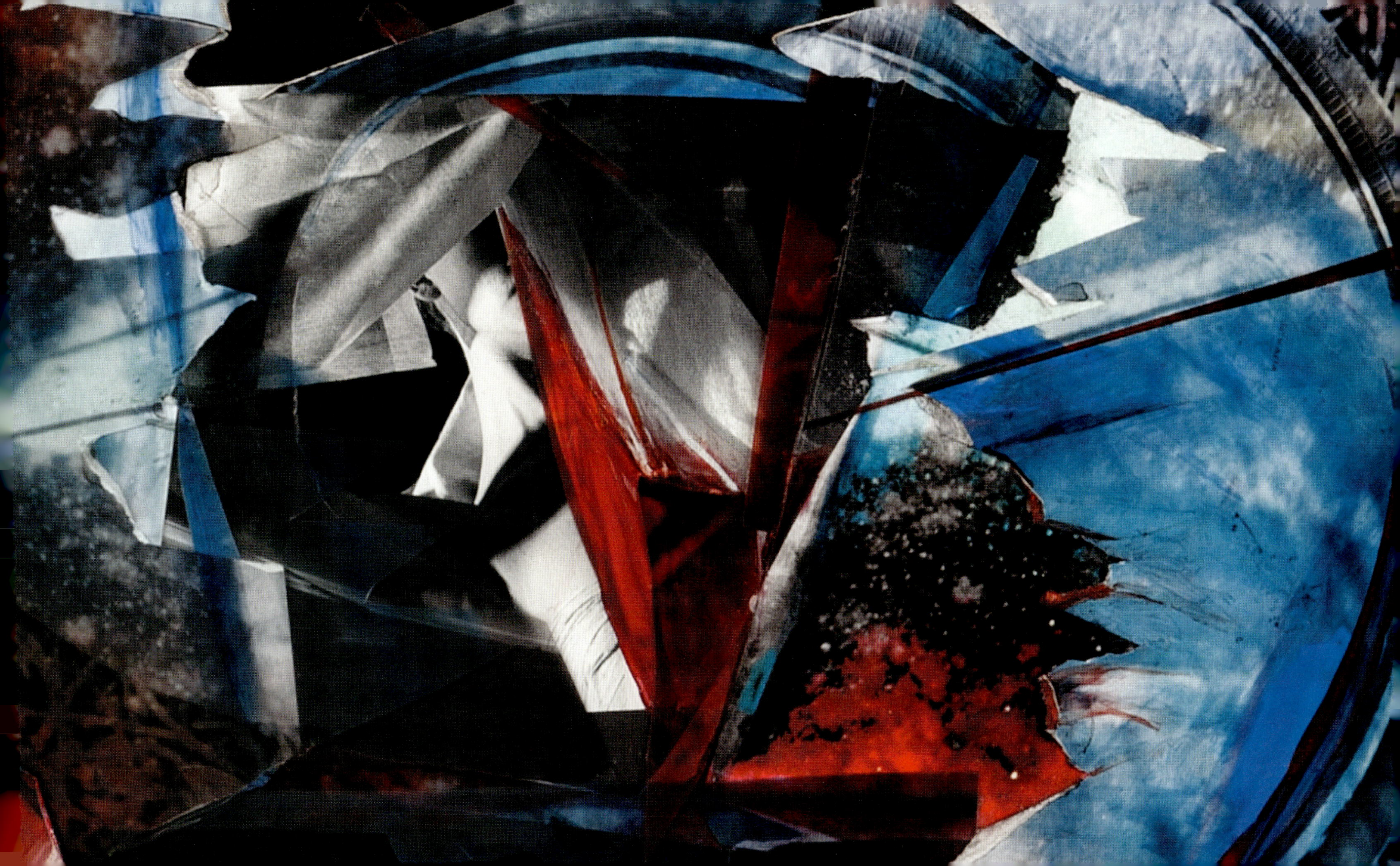

4–11

After this I looked, and, behold, a door was opened in heaven: and the first voice which I heard was as it were of a trumpet talking with me; which said, Come up here, and I will show you things which must be hereafter. And immediately I was in the Spirit: and, behold, a throne was set in heaven, and One sat on the throne. And He that sat was to look upon like a jasper and a sardine stone: and there was a rainbow round about the throne, in sight like unto an emerald.

And round about the throne were four and twenty seats: and upon the seats I saw four and twenty elders sitting, clothed in white raiment; and they had on their heads crowns of gold. And out of the throne proceeded lightnings and thunderings and voices: and there were seven lamps of fire burning before the throne, which are the seven Spirits of God. And before the throne there was a sea of glass like to crystal: and in the midst of the throne, and round about the throne, were four beasts full of eyes before and behind.

And the first beast was like a lion, and the second beast like a calf, and the third beast had a face as a man, and the fourth beast was like a flying eagle. And the four beasts had each of them six wings about him; and they were full of eyes inside: and they rest not day and night, saying, Holy, holy, holy, Lord God Almighty, which was, and is, and is to come. And when those beasts give glory and honor and thanks to Him that sat on the throne, who lives for ever and ever, the four and twenty elders fall down before Him that sat on the throne, and worship Him that lives for ever and ever, and cast their crowns before the throne, saying, You are worthy, O Lord, to receive glory and honor and power: for You have created all things, and for Your pleasure they are and were created.

And I saw in the right hand of Him that sat on the throne a book written inside and on the backside, sealed with seven seals. And I saw a strong angel proclaiming with a loud voice, Who is worthy to open the book, and to loose the seals thereof? And no man in heaven, nor in earth, neither under the earth, was able to open the book, neither to look thereon.

And I wept much, because no man was found worthy to open and to read the book, neither to look thereon.

And one of the elders says to me, Weep not: behold, the Lion of the tribe of Juda, the Root of David, has prevailed to open the book, and to loose the seven seals thereof.

And I beheld, and, lo, in the midst of the throne and of the four beasts, and in the midst of the elders, stood a Lamb as it had been slain, having seven horns and seven eyes, which are the seven Spirits of God sent forth into all the earth. And He came and took the book out of the right hand of Him that sat upon the throne.

And when He had taken the book, the four beasts and four and twenty elders fell down before the Lamb, having every one of them harps, and golden vials full of odors, which are the prayers of saints. And they sung a new song, saying, You are worthy to take the book, and to open the seals thereof: for You were slain, and have redeemed us to God by Your blood out of every kindred, and tongue, and people, and nation; and have made us to our God kings and priests: and we shall reign on the earth.

And I beheld, and I heard the voice of many angels round about the throne and the beasts and the elders: and the number of them was ten thousand times ten thousand, and thousands of thousands; saying with a loud voice, Worthy is the Lamb that was slain to receive power, and riches, and wisdom, and strength, and honor, and glory, and blessing.

And every creature which is in heaven, and on the earth, and under the earth, and such as are in the sea, and all that are in them, heard I saying, Blessing, and honor, and glory, and power, be unto Him that sits upon the throne, and to the Lamb for ever and ever. And the four beasts said, Amen. And the four and twenty elders fell down and worshiped Him that lives for ever and ever.

And I saw when the Lamb opened one of the seals, and I heard, as it were the noise of thunder, one of the four beasts saying, Come and see. And I saw, and behold a white horse: and he that sat on him had a bow; and a crown was given unto him: and he went forth conquering, and to conquer.

And when He had opened the second seal, I heard the second beast say, Come and see. And there went out another horse that was red: and power was given to him that sat thereon to take peace from the earth, and that they should kill one another: and there was given to him a great sword.

And when He had opened the third seal, I heard the third beast say, Come and see. And I beheld, and lo a black horse; and he that sat on him had a pair of balances in his hand. And I heard a voice in the midst of the four beasts say, A measure of wheat for a penny, and three measures of barley for a penny; and see you hurt not the oil and the wine.

And when He had opened the fourth seal, I heard the voice of the fourth beast say, Come and see. And I looked, and behold a pale horse: and his name that sat on him was Death, and Hell followed with him. And power was given to them over the fourth part of the earth, to kill with sword, and with hunger, and with death, and with the beasts of the earth.

And when He had opened the fifth seal, I saw under the altar the souls of them that were slain for the word of God, and for the testimony which they held: And they cried with a loud voice, saying, How long, O Lord, holy and true, do You not judge and avenge our blood on them that dwell on the earth? And white robes were given to every one of them; and it was said unto them, that they should rest yet for a little season, until their fellow-servants also and their brethren, that should be killed as they were, should be fulfilled.

And I beheld when He had opened the sixth seal, and, lo, there was a great earthquake; and the sun became black as sackcloth of hair, and the moon became as blood; and the stars of heaven fell to the earth, even as a fig tree casts her untimely figs, when she is shaken of a mighty wind. And the heaven departed as a scroll when it is rolled together; and every mountain and island were moved out of their places.

And the kings of the earth, and the great men, and the rich men, and the chief captains, and the mighty men, and every bondman, and every free man, hid themselves in the dens and in the rocks of the mountains; and said to the mountains and rocks, Fall on us, and hide us from the face of Him that sits on the throne, and from the wrath of the Lamb: for the great day of His wrath is come; and who shall be able to stand?

And after these things I saw four angels standing on the four corners of the earth, holding the four winds of the earth, that the wind should not blow on the earth, nor on the sea, nor on any tree.

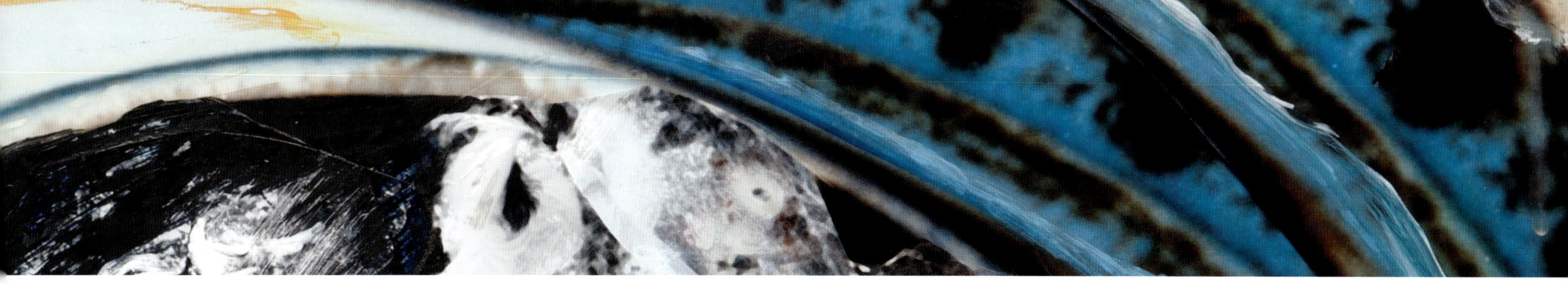

And I saw another angel ascending from the east, having the seal of the living God: and he cried with a loud voice to the four angels, to whom it was given to hurt the earth and the sea, saying, Hurt not the earth, neither the sea, nor the trees, till we have sealed the servants of our God in their foreheads.

And I heard the number of them which were sealed: and there were sealed a hundred and forty and four thousand of all the tribes of the children of Israel. Of the tribe of Juda were sealed twelve thousand. Of the tribe of Reuben were sealed twelve thousand. Of the tribe of Gad were sealed twelve thousand. Of the tribe of Aser were sealed twelve thousand. Of the tribe of Nepthalim were sealed twelve thousand. Of the tribe of Manasses were sealed twelve thousand. Of the tribe of Simeon were sealed twelve thousand. Of the tribe of Levi were sealed twelve thousand. Of the tribe of Issachar were sealed twelve thousand. Of the tribe of Zabulon were sealed twelve thousand. Of the tribe of Joseph were sealed twelve thousand. Of the tribe of Benjamin were sealed twelve thousand.

After this I beheld, and, lo, a great multitude, which no man could number, of all nations, and kindreds, and people, and tongues, stood before the throne, and before the Lamb, clothed with white robes, and palms in their hands; and cried with a loud voice, saying, Salvation to our God which sits upon the throne, and to the Lamb.

And all the angels stood round about the throne, and about the elders and the four beasts, and fell before the throne on their faces, and worshiped God, saying, Amen: Blessing, and glory, and wisdom, and thanksgiving, and honor, and power, and might, be to our God for ever and ever. Amen.

And one of the elders answered, saying to me, What are these which are arrayed in white robes? and from where came they? And I said unto him, Sir, you know. And he said to me, These are they which came out of great tribulation, and have washed their robes, and made them white in the blood of the Lamb. Therefore are they before the throne of God, and serve Him day and night in His temple: and He that sits on the throne shall dwell among them. They shall hunger no more, neither thirst any more; neither shall the sun light on them, nor any heat. For the Lamb which is in the midst of the throne shall feed them, and shall lead them to living fountains of waters: and God shall wipe away all tears from their eyes.

And when He had opened the seventh seal, there was silence in heaven about the space of half an hour.

And I saw the seven angels which stood before God; and to them were given seven trumpets. And another angel came and stood at the altar, having a golden censer; and there was given unto him much incense, that he should offer it with the prayers of all saints upon the golden altar which was before the throne. And the smoke of the incense, which came with the prayers of the saints, ascended up before God out of the angel's hand. And the angel took the censer, and filled it with fire of the altar, and cast it into the earth: and there were voices, and thunderings, and lightnings, and an earthquake.

And the seven angels which had the seven trumpets prepared themselves to sound. The first angel sounded, and there followed hail and fire mingled with blood, and they were cast upon the earth: and the third part of trees was burned up, and all green grass was burned up. And the second angel sounded, and as it were a great mountain burning with fire was cast into the sea: and the third part of the sea became blood; and the third part of the creatures which were in the sea, and had life, died; and the third part of the ships were destroyed.

And the third angel sounded, and there fell a great star from heaven, burning as it were a lamp, and it fell upon the third part of the rivers, and upon the fountains of waters; and the name of the star is called Wormwood: and the third part of the waters became wormwood; and many men died of the waters, because they were made bitter. And the fourth angel sounded, and the third part of the sun was smitten, and the third part of the moon, and the third part of the stars; so as the third part of them was darkened, and the day shone not for a third part of it, and the night likewise.

And I beheld, and heard an angel flying through the midst of heaven, saying with a loud voice, Woe, woe, woe, to the inhabiters of the earth by reason of the other voices of the trumpet of the three angels, which are yet to sound!

And the fifth angel sounded, and I saw a star fall from heaven unto the earth: and to him was given the key of the bottomless pit. And he opened the bottomless pit; and there arose a smoke out of the pit, as the smoke of a great furnace; and the sun and the air were darkened by reason of the smoke of the pit.

And there came out of the smoke locusts upon the earth: and to them was given power, as the scorpions of the earth have power. And it was commanded them that they should not hurt the grass of the earth, neither any green thing, neither any tree; but only those men which have not the seal of God in their foreheads. And to them it was given that they should not kill them, but that they should be tormented five months: and their torment was as the torment of a scorpion, when he strikes a man. And in those days shall men seek death, and shall not find it; and shall desire to die, and death shall flee from them.

And the shapes of the locusts were like to horses prepared to battle; and on their heads were as it were crowns like gold, and their faces were as the faces of men. And they had hair as the hair of women, and their teeth were as the teeth of lions. And they had breastplates, as it were breastplates of iron; and the sound of their wings was as the sound of chariots of many horses running to battle. And they had tails like to scorpions, and there were stings in their tails: and their power was to hurt men five months. And they had a king over them, which is the angel of the bottomless pit, whose name in the Hebrew tongue is Abaddon, but in the Greek tongue has his name Apollyon.

One woe is past; and, behold, there come two woes more hereafter.

And the sixth angel sounded, and I heard a voice from the four horns of the golden altar which is before God, saying to the sixth angel which had the trumpet, Loose the four angels which are bound in the great river Euphrates. And the four angels were loosed, which were prepared for an hour, and a day, and a month, and a year, for to slay the third part of men.

And the number of the army of the horsemen were two hundred thousand thousand: and I heard the number of them. And thus I saw the horses in the vision, and them that sat on them, having breastplates of fire, and of jacinth, and brimstone:

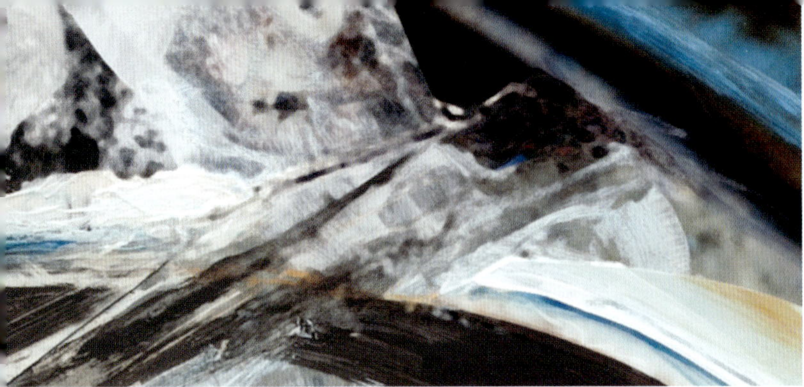

and the heads of the horses were as the heads of lions; and out of their mouths issued fire and smoke and brimstone.

By these three was the third part of men killed, by the fire, and by the smoke, and by the brimstone, which issued out of their mouths. For their power is in their mouth, and in their tails: for their tails were like to serpents, and had heads, and with them they do hurt.

And the rest of the men which were not killed by these plagues yet repented not of the works of their hands, that they should not worship devils, and idols of gold, and silver, and brass, and stone, and of wood: which neither can see, nor hear, nor walk: neither repented they of their murders, nor of their sorceries, nor of their fornication, nor of their thefts.

And I saw another mighty angel come down from heaven, clothed with a cloud: and a rainbow was upon his head, and his face was as it were the sun, and his feet as pillars of fire: and he had in his hand a little book open: and he set his right foot upon the sea, and his left foot on the earth, and cried with a loud voice, as when a lion roars: and when he had cried, seven thunders uttered their voices.

And when the seven thunders had uttered their voices, I was about to write: and I heard a voice from heaven saying unto me, Seal up those things which the seven thunders uttered, and write them not.

And the angel which I saw stand upon the sea and upon the earth lifted up his hand to heaven, and swore by Him that lives for ever and ever, who created heaven, and the things that therein are, and the earth, and the things that therein

are, and the sea, and the things which are therein, that there should be time no longer:

But in the days of the voice of the seventh angel, when he shall begin to sound, the mystery of God should be finished, as He has declared to His servants the prophets. And the voice which I heard from heaven spoke to me again, and said, Go and take the little book which is open in the hand of the angel which stands upon the sea and upon the earth.

And I went unto the angel, and said to him, Give me the little book. And he said to me, Take it, and eat it up; and it shall make your belly bitter, but it shall be in your mouth sweet as honey. And I took the little book out of the angel's hand, and ate it up; and it was in my mouth sweet as honey: and as soon as I had eaten it, my belly was bitter.

And he said to me, You must prophesy again before many peoples, and nations, and tongues, and kings.

And there was given me a reed like unto a rod: and the angel stood, saying, Rise, and measure the temple of God, and the altar, and them that worship therein. But the court which is outside the temple leave out, and measure it not; for it is given to the Gentiles: and the holy city shall they tread under foot forty and two months. And I will give power to my two witnesses, and they shall prophesy a thousand two hundred and threescore days, clothed in sackcloth. These are the two olive trees, and the two candlesticks standing before the God of the earth. And if any man will hurt them, fire proceeds out of their mouth, and devours their enemies: and if any man will hurt them, he must in this manner be killed. These have power

to shut heaven, that it rain not in the days of their prophecy: and have power over waters to turn them to blood, and to smite the earth with all plagues, as often as they will.

And when they shall have finished their testimony, the beast that ascends out of the bottomless pit shall make war against them, and shall overcome them, and kill them. And their dead bodies shall lie in the street of the great city, which spiritually is called Sodom and Egypt, where also our Lord was crucified. And they of the people and kindreds and tongues and nations shall see their dead bodies three days and an half, and shall not permit their dead bodies to be put in graves. And they that dwell upon the earth shall rejoice over them, and make merry, and shall send gifts one to another; because these two prophets tormented them that dwelt on the earth.

And after three days and a half the Spirit of life from God entered into them, and they stood upon their feet; and great fear fell upon them which saw them. And they heard a great voice from heaven saying to them, Come up here. And they ascended up to heaven in a cloud; and their enemies beheld them.

And the same hour was there a great earthquake, and the tenth part of the city fell, and in the earthquake were slain of men seven thousand: and the remnant were frightened, and gave glory to the God of heaven.

The second woe is past; and, behold, the third woe comes quickly.

And the seventh angel sounded; and there were great voices in heaven, saying, The kingdoms of this world are

become the kingdoms of our Lord, and of His Christ; and He shall reign for ever and ever.

And the four and twenty elders, which sat before God on their seats, fell upon their faces, and worshiped God, saying, We give You thanks, O Lord God Almighty, which are, and were, and are to come; because You have taken to You Your great power, and have reigned. And the nations were angry, and Your wrath is come, and the time of the dead, that they should be judged, and that You should give reward to Your servants the prophets, and to the saints, and them that fear Your name, small and great; and should destroy them which destroy the earth.

And the temple of God was opened in heaven, and there was seen in His temple the ark of His testament: and there were lightnings, and voices, and thunderings, and an earthquake, and great hail.

And the nations were angry, and Thy wrath is come, and the time of the dead, that they should be judged, and that Thou shouldest give reward unto Thy servants the prophets, and to the saints, and them that fear Thy name, small and great; and shouldest destroy them which destroy the earth.

And the temple of God was opened in heaven, and there was seen in His temple the ark of His testament: and there were lightnings, and voices, and thunderings, and an earthquake, and great hail.

ROOM 3

EXPLORING HEAVEN

Jesus returns to restore all things to their beautiful, original state.

"Behold, a door was opened in heaven" (Revelation 4:1).

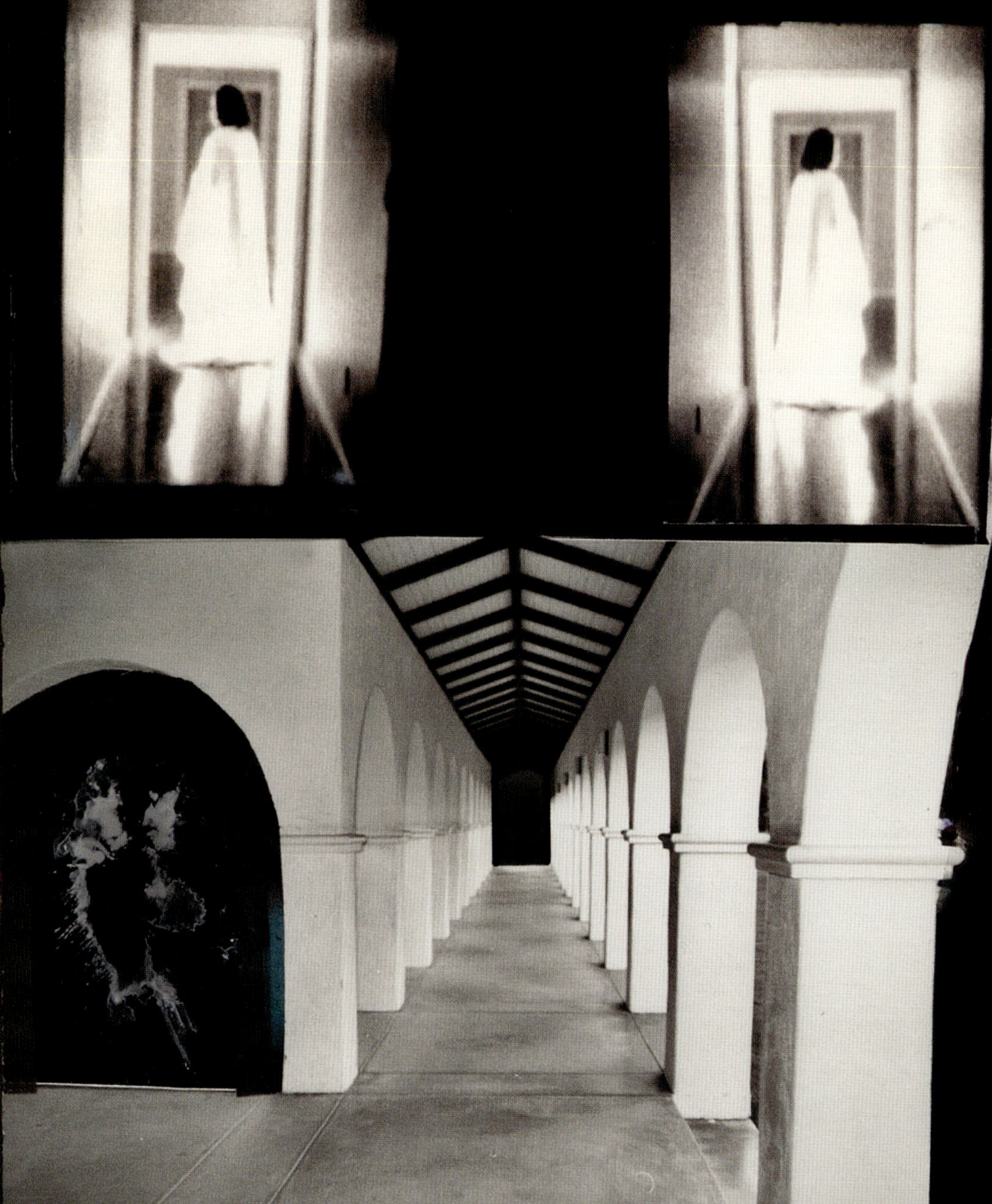

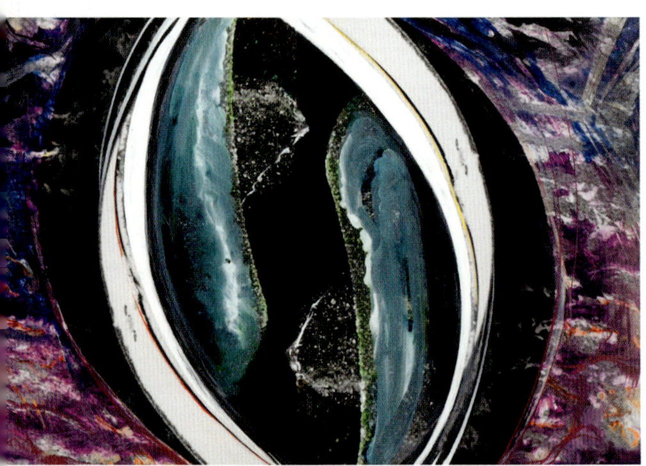

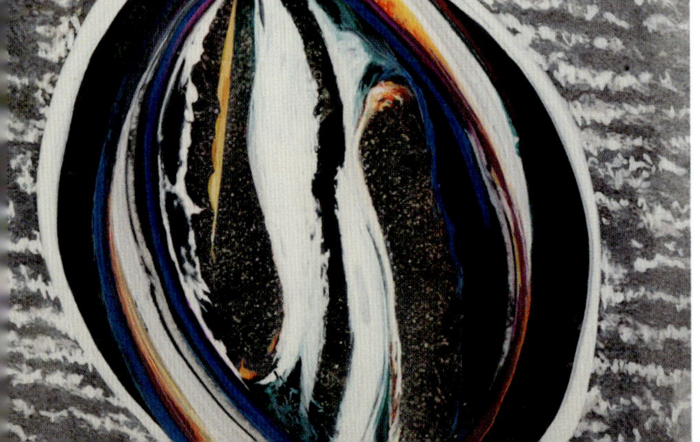

3 DIMENSIONS OF MAN

THIS SHOWS HOW BALANCE AND DEVELOPMENT AMONG BODY, SOUL,
AND SPIRIT ARE VITAL TO ACHIEVING A HARMONIOUS LIFE.

Everyone desires wholeness, and we are made whole in Him.

The body, soul, and spirit are perfected in heaven.

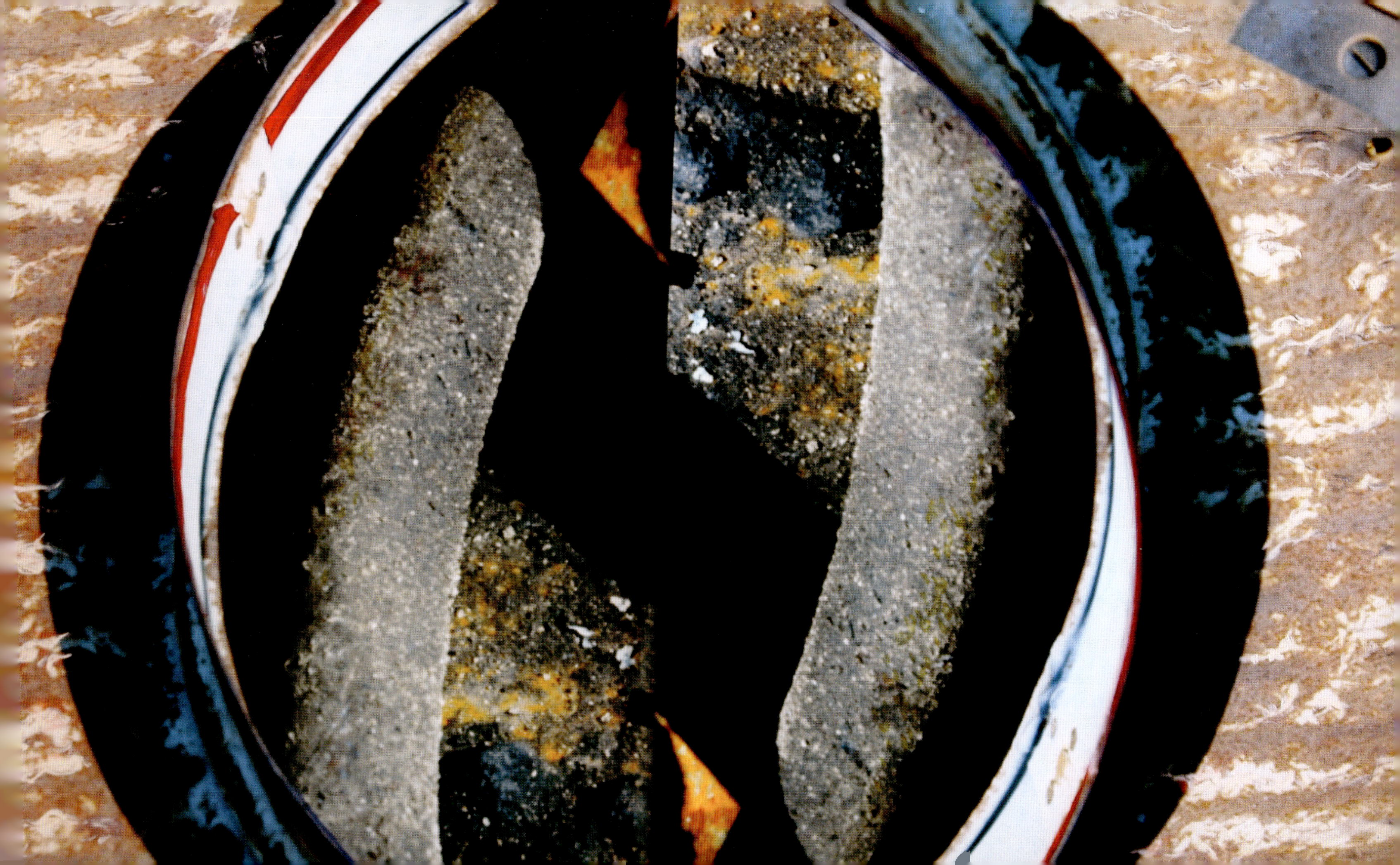

LOOKING AT CONFUSION

THE PERSPECTIVE OF THIS WORK, AS WELL AS THIS PORTION OF REVELATION,
IS TOP-DOWN.

A heavenly viewpoint of the ugliness clashing here on earth.

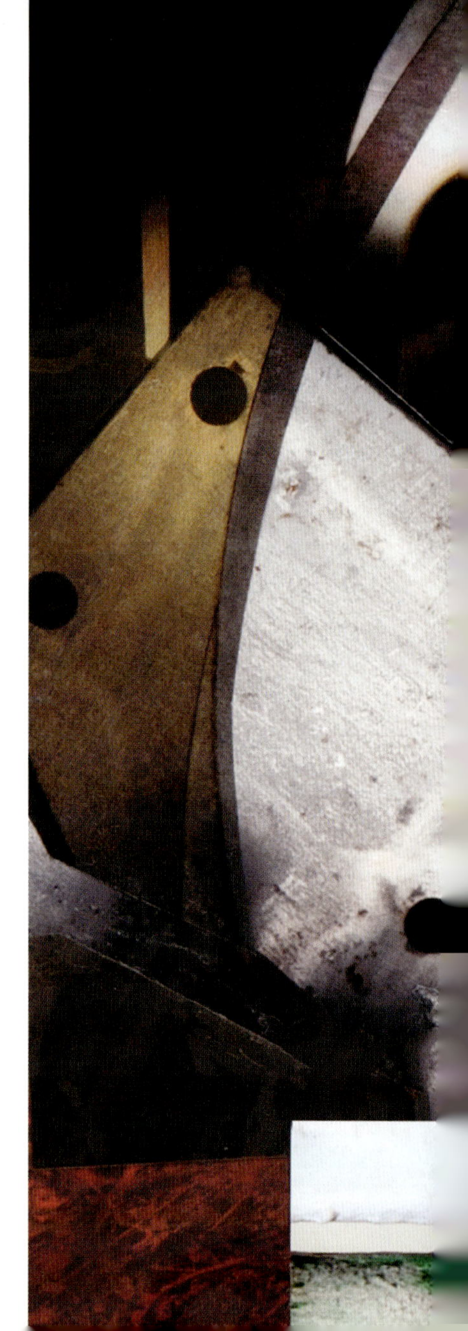

*"An angel flying through the midst of heaven,
saying with a loud voice, Woe, woe, woe"* (Revelation 8:13).

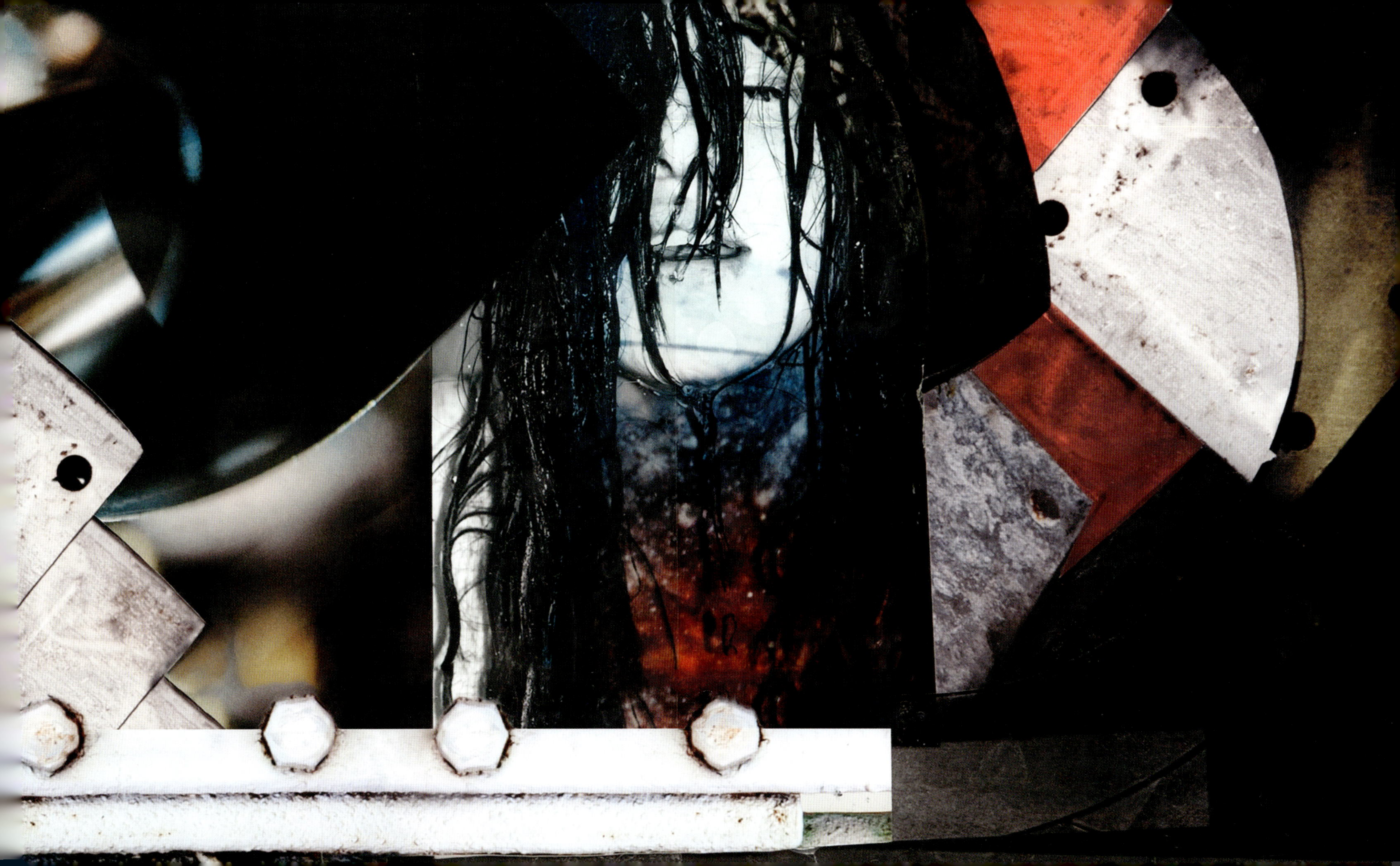

BELOVED SLEEP

THIS PIECE EVOKES TRANQUILITY, AS IF THE VIEWER IS FLOATING ON WATER.

Only He gives excellent rest.

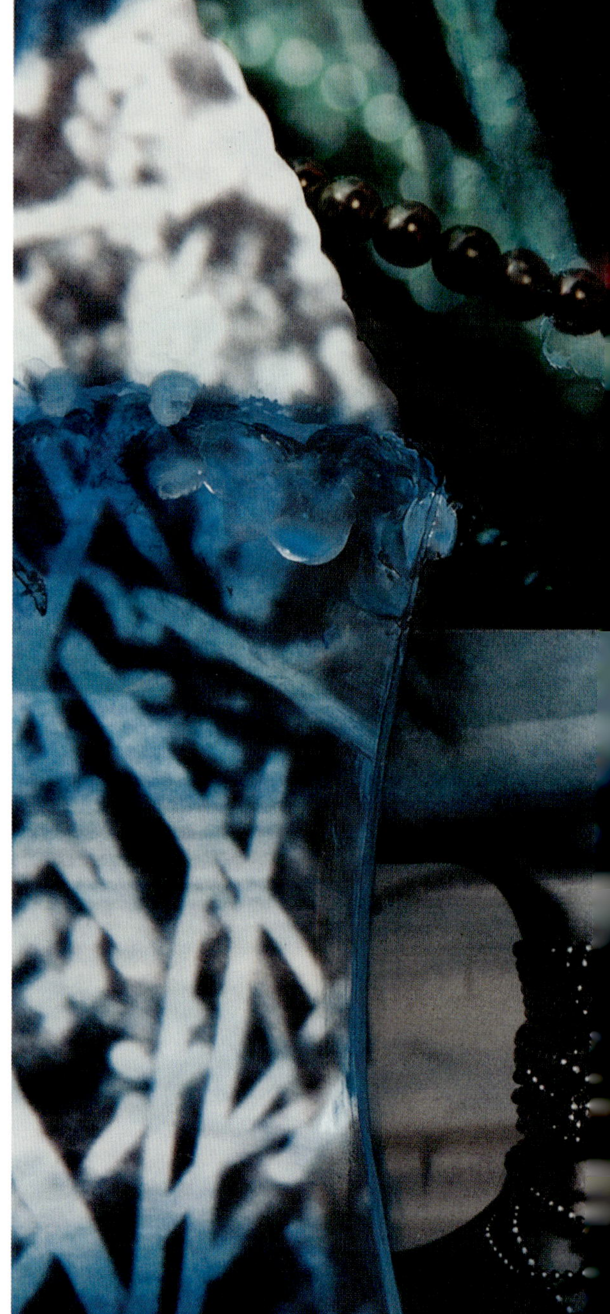

"Rest yet for a little season" (Revelation 6:11).

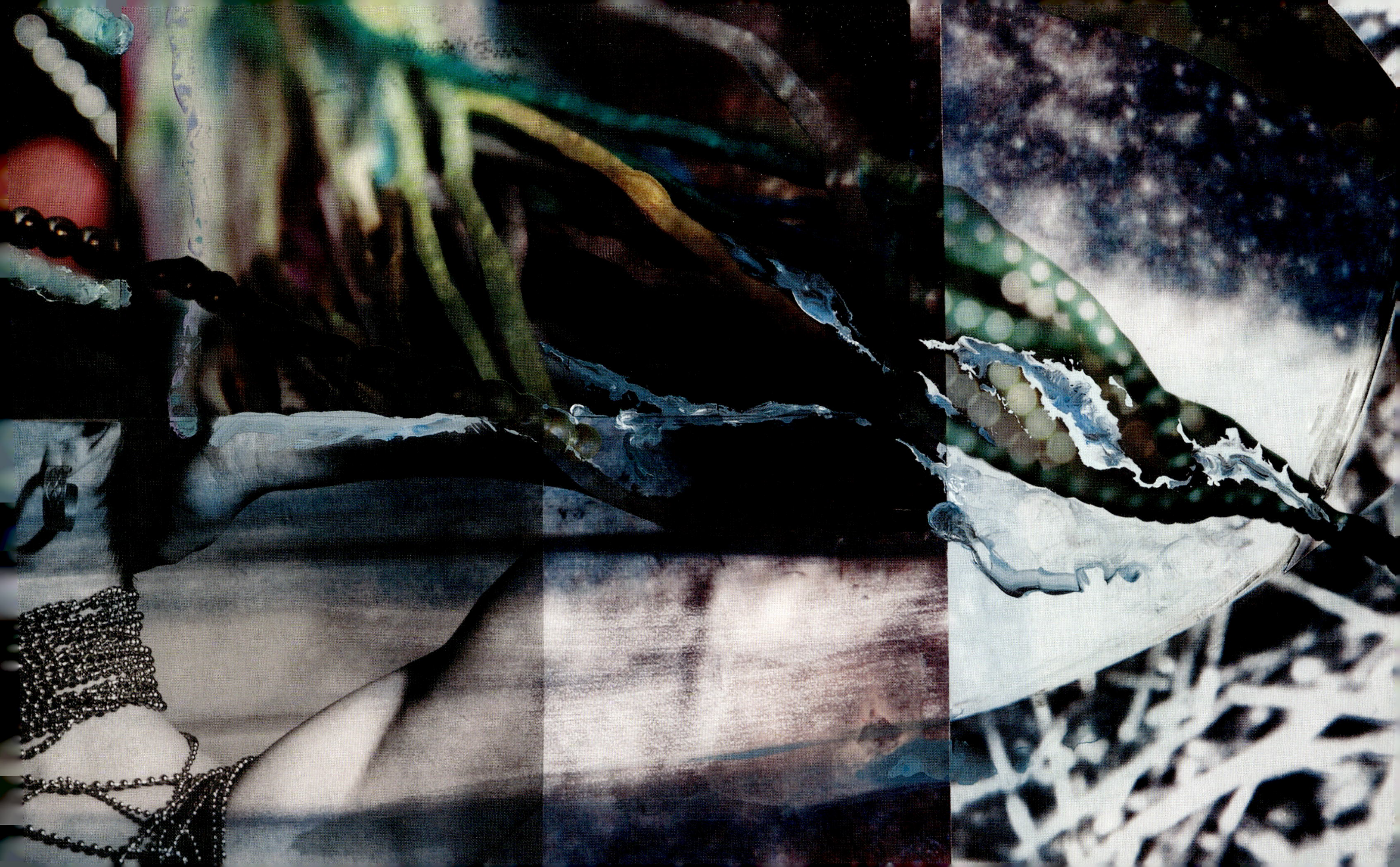

PERFECT RHYTHM

Only Jesus is worthy of our praise.

"And they sung a new song, saying, You are worthy to take the book, and to open the seals thereof: for You were slain, and have redeemed us to God by Your blood out of every kindred, and tongue, and people, and nation" (Revelation 5:9).

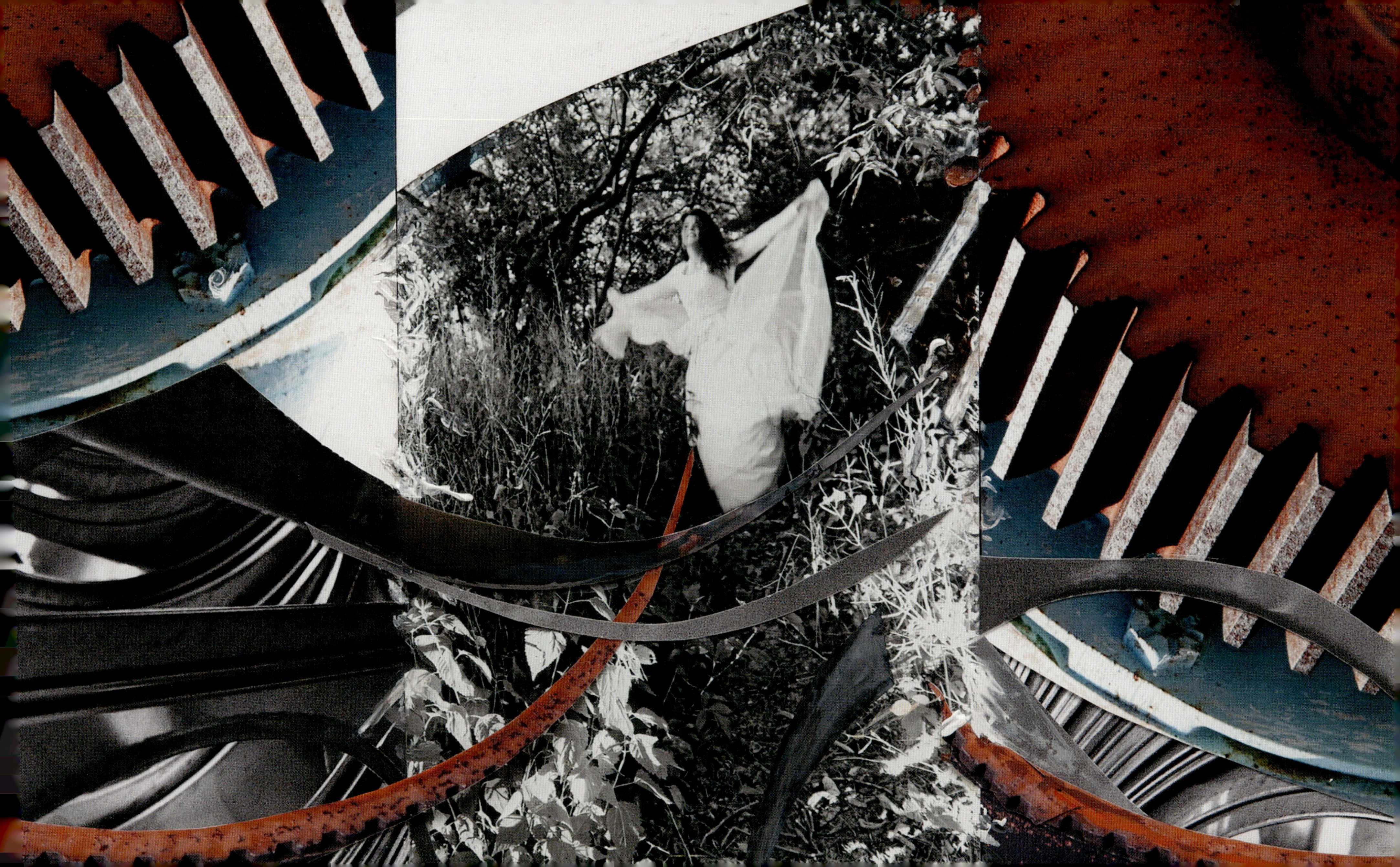

STEADFAST

The world is in chaos. The church stands strong.

Jesus is on the throne.

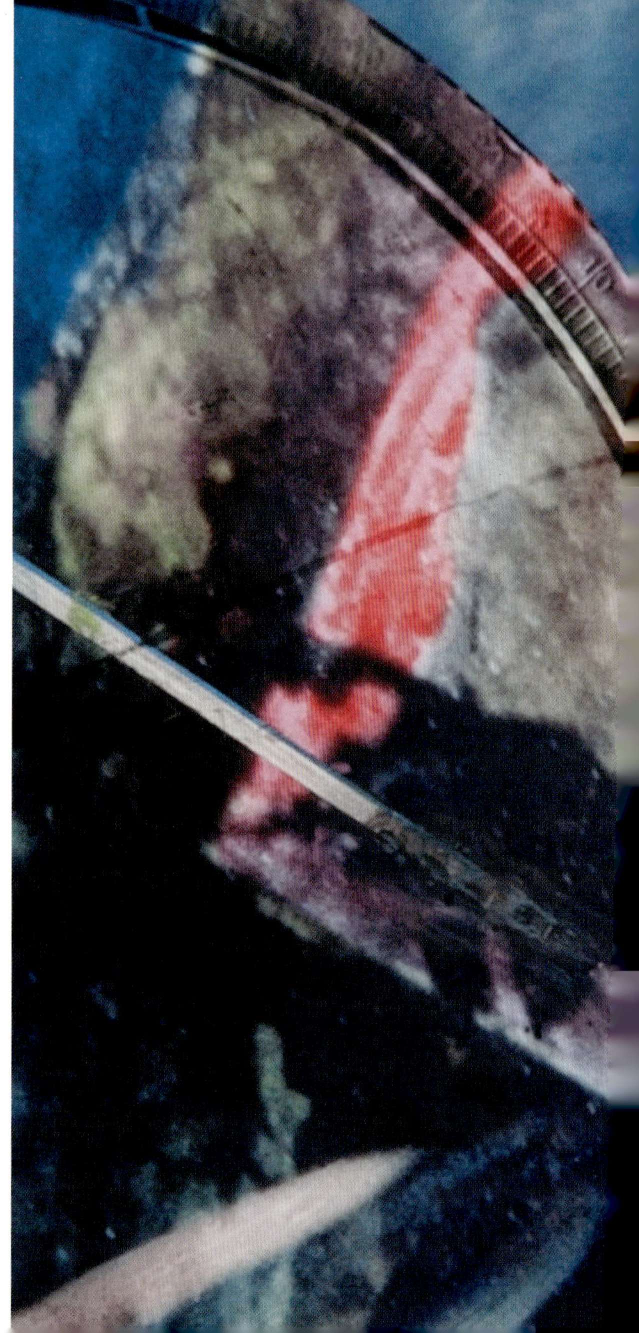

"Behold, a throne was set in heaven, and One sat on the throne. And He that sat was to look upon like a jasper and a sardine stone: and there was a rainbow round about the throne, in sight like to an emerald" (Revelation 4:2–3).

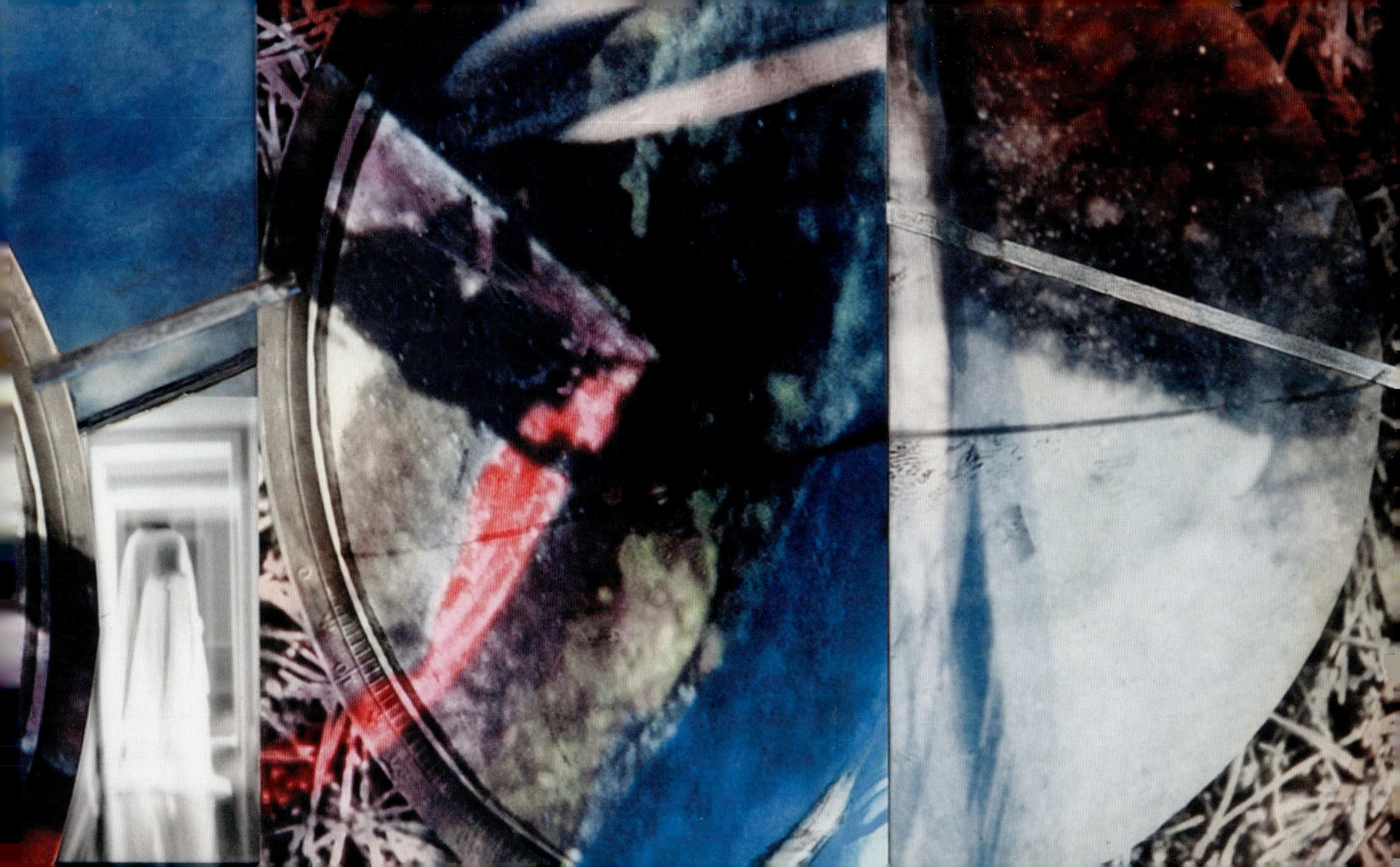

TAKING FLIGHT

RESURRECTION FOLLOWS THE OPENING OF THE SIXTH SEAL.

The door to heaven opens, and we take flight. The trumpets and voices accompany us,
but only because the blood of Jesus opened that door.

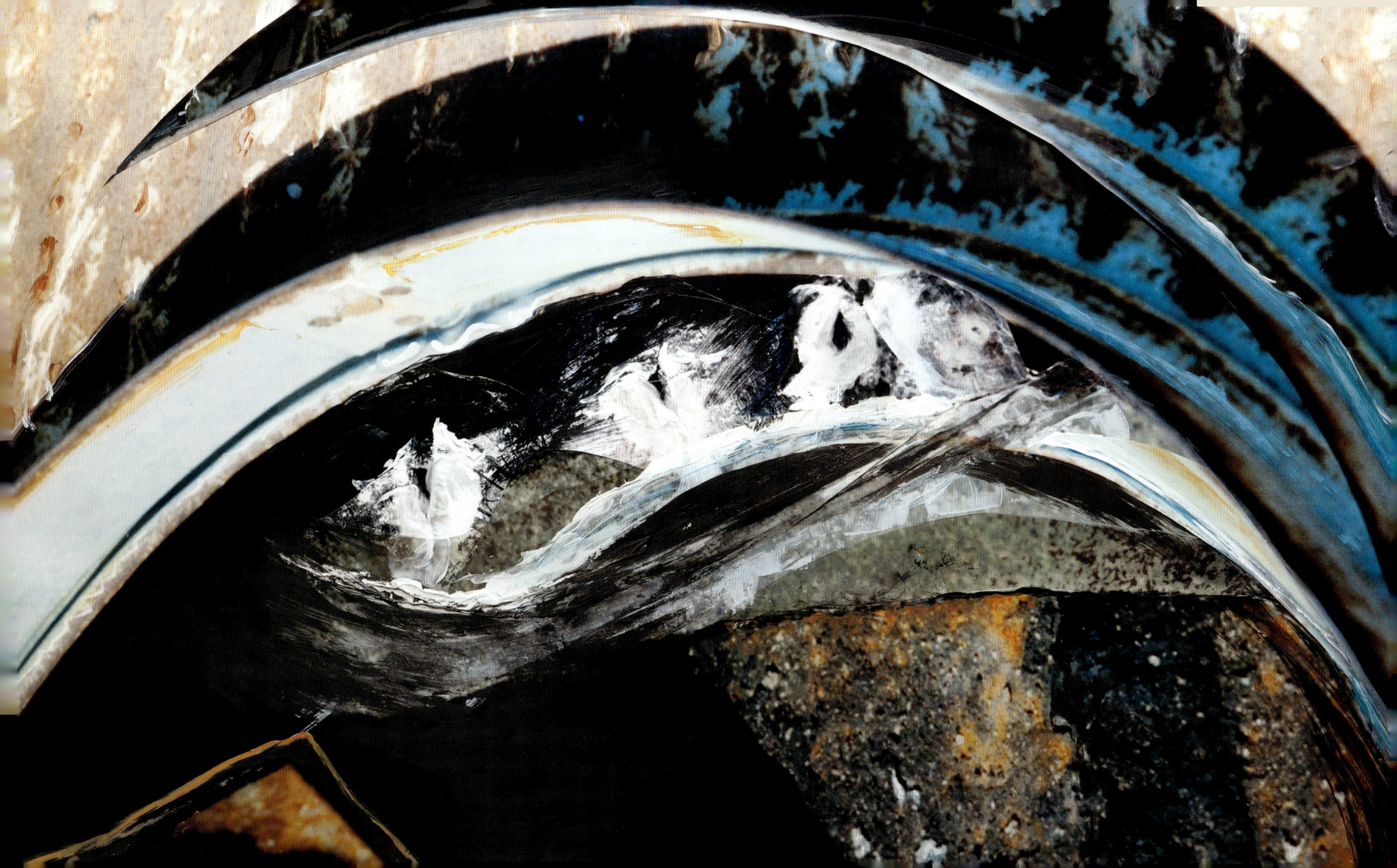

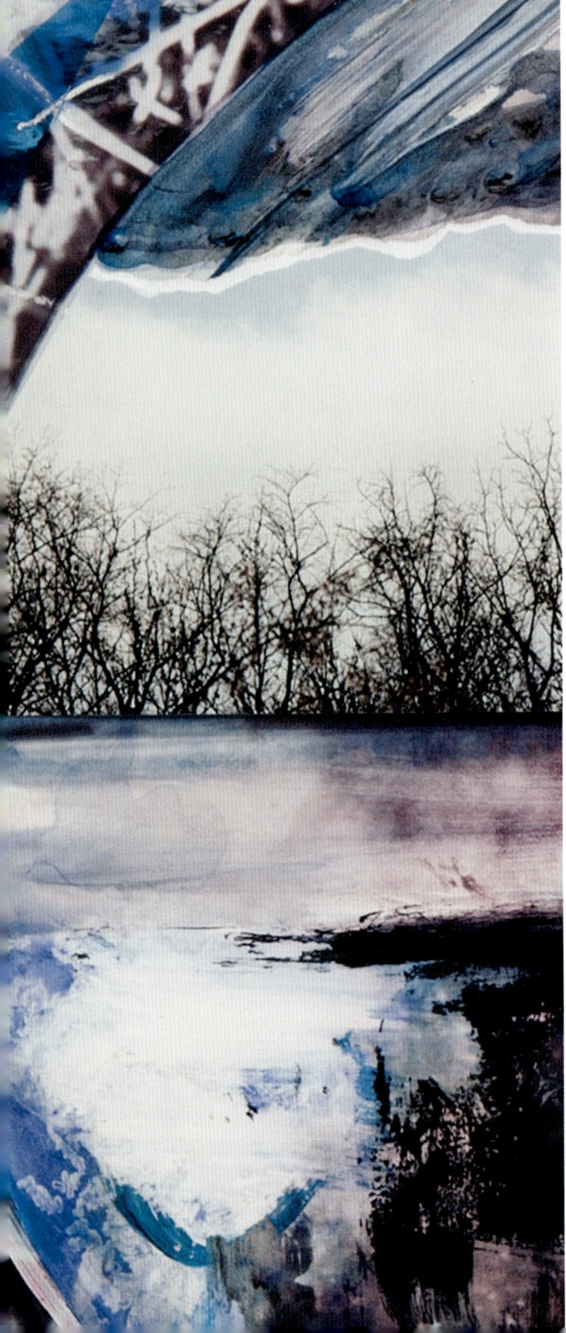

12–16

And there appeared a great wonder in heaven; a woman clothed with the sun, and the moon under her feet, and upon her head a crown of twelve stars: and she being with child cried, travailing in birth, and pained to be delivered.

And there appeared another wonder in heaven; and behold a great red dragon, having seven heads and ten horns, and seven crowns upon his heads. And his tail drew the third part of the stars of heaven, and did cast them to the earth: and the dragon stood before the woman which was ready to be delivered, for to devour her child as soon as it was born.

And she brought forth a man child, who was to rule all nations with a rod of iron: and her child was caught up to God, and to His throne. And the woman fled into the wilderness, where she has a place prepared of God, that they should feed her there a thousand two hundred and threescore days.

And there was war in heaven: Michael and his angels fought against the dragon; and the dragon fought and his angels, and prevailed not; neither was their place found any more in heaven. And the great dragon was cast out, that old serpent, called the Devil, and Satan, which deceives the whole world: he was cast out into the earth, and his angels were cast out with him.

And I heard a loud voice saying in heaven, Now is come salvation, and strength, and the kingdom of our God, and the power of His Christ: for the accuser of our brethren is cast down, which accused them before our God day and night.

And they overcame him by the blood of the Lamb, and by the word of their testimony; and they loved not their lives unto the death. Therefore rejoice, you heavens, and you that dwell in them. Woe to the inhabiters of the earth and of the sea! for the devil is come down to you, having great wrath, because he knows that he has but a short time.

And when the dragon saw that he was cast to the earth, he persecuted the woman which brought forth the man child. And to the woman were given two wings of a great eagle, that she might fly into the wilderness, into her place, where she is nourished for a time, and times, and half a time, from the face of the serpent.

And the serpent cast out of his mouth water as a flood after the woman, that he might cause her to be carried away of the flood. And the earth helped the woman, and the earth opened her mouth, and swallowed up the flood which the dragon cast out of his mouth.

And the dragon was angry with the woman, and went to make war with the remnant of her seed, which keep the commandments of God, and have the testimony of Jesus Christ.

And I stood upon the sand of the sea, and saw a beast rise up out of the sea, having seven heads and ten horns, and upon his horns ten crowns, and upon his heads the name of blasphemy. And the beast which I saw was like to a leopard, and his feet were as the feet of a bear, and his mouth as the mouth of a lion: and the dragon gave him his power, and his seat, and great authority. And I saw one of his heads as it were wounded to death; and his deadly wound was healed: and all the world wondered after the beast.

And they worshiped the dragon which gave power to the beast: and they worshiped the beast, saying, Who is like to the beast? who is able to make war with him? And there was given to him a mouth speaking great things and blasphemies; and power was given to him to continue forty and two months. And he opened his mouth in blasphemy against God, to blaspheme His name, and His tabernacle, and them that dwell in heaven.

And it was given to him to make war with the saints, and to overcome them: and power was given him over all kindreds, and tongues, and nations. And all that dwell upon the earth shall worship him, whose names are not written in the book of life of the Lamb slain from the foundation of the world.

If any man have an ear, let him hear. He that leads into captivity shall go into captivity: he that kills with the sword must be killed with the sword. Here is the patience and the faith of the saints.

And I beheld another beast coming up out of the earth; and he had two horns like a lamb, and he spoke as a dragon. And he exercises all the power of the first beast before him, and causes the earth and them which dwell therein to worship the first beast, whose deadly wound was healed. And he does great wonders, so that he makes fire come down from heaven on the earth in the sight of men, and deceives them that dwell on the earth by the means of those miracles which he had power to do in the sight of the beast; saying to them that dwell on the earth, that they should make an image to the beast, which had the wound by a sword, and did live.

And he had power to give life to the image of the beast, that the image of the beast should both speak, and cause that as many as would not worship the image of the beast should be killed. And he causes all, both small and great, rich and poor, free and bond, to receive a mark in their right hand, or in their foreheads: And that no man might buy or sell, save he that had the mark, or the name of the beast, or the number of his name.

Here is wisdom. Let him that has understanding count the number of the beast: for it is the number of a man; and his number is Six hundred threescore and six.

And I looked, and, lo, a Lamb stood on the mount Zion, and with Him a hundred forty and four thousand, having His Father's name written in their foreheads. And I heard a voice from heaven, as the voice of many waters, and as the voice of a great thunder: and I heard the voice of harpers harping with their harps: and they sung as it were a new song before the throne, and before the four beasts, and the elders: and no man could learn that song but the hundred and forty and four thousand, which were redeemed from the earth.

These are they which were not defiled with women; for they are virgins. These are they which follow the Lamb wherever He goes. These were redeemed from among men, being the first-fruits to God and to the Lamb. And in their mouth was found no guile: for they are without fault before the throne of God.

And I saw another angel fly in the midst of heaven, having the everlasting gospel to preach to them that dwell on the earth, and to every nation, and kindred, and tongue, and people, saying with a loud voice, Fear God, and give glory to Him; for the hour of His judgment is come: and worship Him that made heaven, and earth, and the sea, and the fountains of waters.

And there followed another angel, saying, Babylon is fallen, is fallen, that great city, because she made all nations drink of the wine of the wrath of her fornication. And the third angel followed them, saying with a loud voice, If any man worship the beast and his image, and receive his mark in his forehead, or in his hand, the same shall drink of the wine of the wrath of God, which is poured out without mixture into the cup of His indignation; and he shall be tormented with fire and brimstone in the presence of the holy angels, and in the presence of the Lamb: and the smoke of their torment ascends up for ever and ever: and they have no rest day nor night, who worship the beast and his image, and whosoever receives the mark of his name.

Here is the patience of the saints: here are they that keep the commandments of God, and the faith of Jesus.

And I heard a voice from heaven saying to me, Write, Blessed are the dead which die in the Lord from henceforth: Yea, says the Spirit, that they may rest from their labors; and their works do follow them. And I looked, and behold a white cloud, and upon the cloud one sat like to the Son of man, having on His head a golden crown, and in His hand a sharp sickle.

And another angel came out of the temple, crying with a loud voice to Him that sat on the cloud, Thrust in Your sickle, and reap: for the time is come for You to reap; for the harvest of the earth is ripe.

And He that sat on the cloud thrust in His sickle on the earth; and the earth was reaped.

And another angel came out of the temple which is in heaven, he also having a sharp sickle. And another angel came out from the altar, which had power over fire; and cried with a loud cry to him that had the sharp sickle, saying, Thrust in thy sharp sickle, and gather the clusters of the vine of the earth; for her grapes are fully ripe.

And the angel thrust in his sickle into the earth, and gathered the vine of the earth, and cast it into the great winepress of the wrath of God. And the winepress was trodden without the city, and blood came out of the winepress, even to the horse bridles, by the space of a thousand and six hundred furlongs.

And I saw another sign in heaven, great and marvellous, seven angels having the seven last plagues; for in them is filled up the wrath of God. And I saw as it were a sea of glass mingled with fire: and them that had gotten the victory over the beast, and over his image, and over his mark, and over the number of his name, stand on the sea of glass, having the harps of God. And they sing the song of Moses the servant of God, and the song of the Lamb, saying, Great and marvellous are Your works, Lord God Almighty; just and true are Your ways, You King of saints. Who shall not fear You, O Lord, and glorify Your name? for You only are holy: for all nations shall come and worship before You; for Your judgments are made manifest.

And after that I looked, and, behold, the temple of the tabernacle of the testimony in heaven was opened: and the seven angels came out of the temple, having the seven plagues, clothed in pure and white linen, and having their breasts girded with golden girdles. And one of the four beasts gave to the seven angels seven golden vials full of the wrath of God, who lives for ever and ever. And the temple was filled

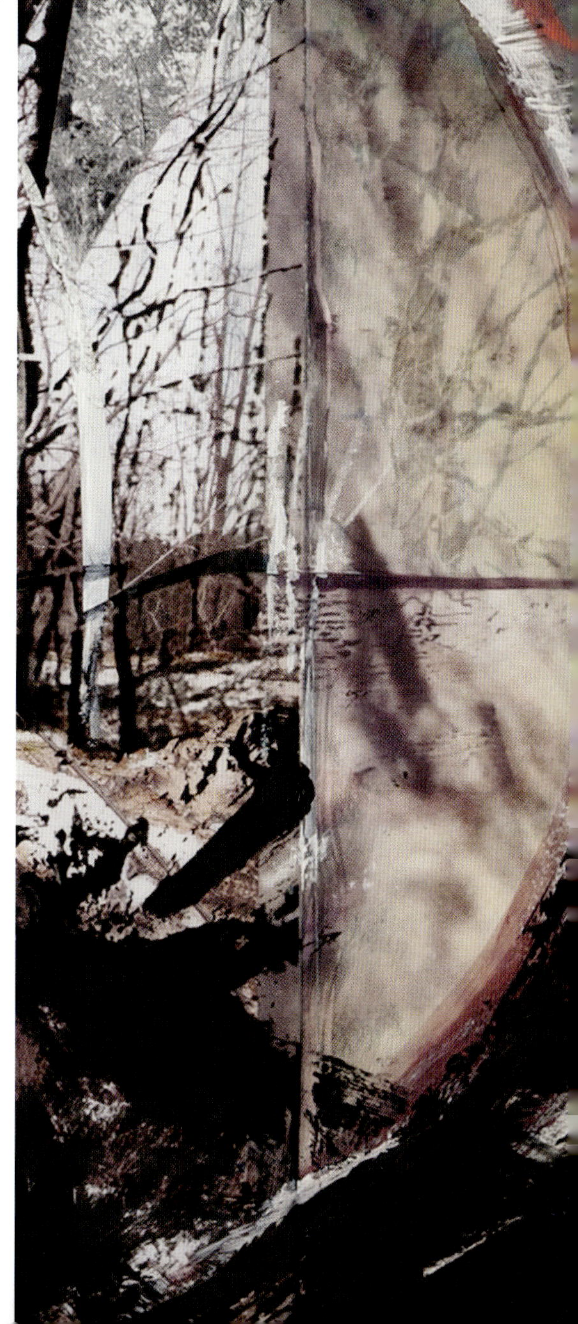

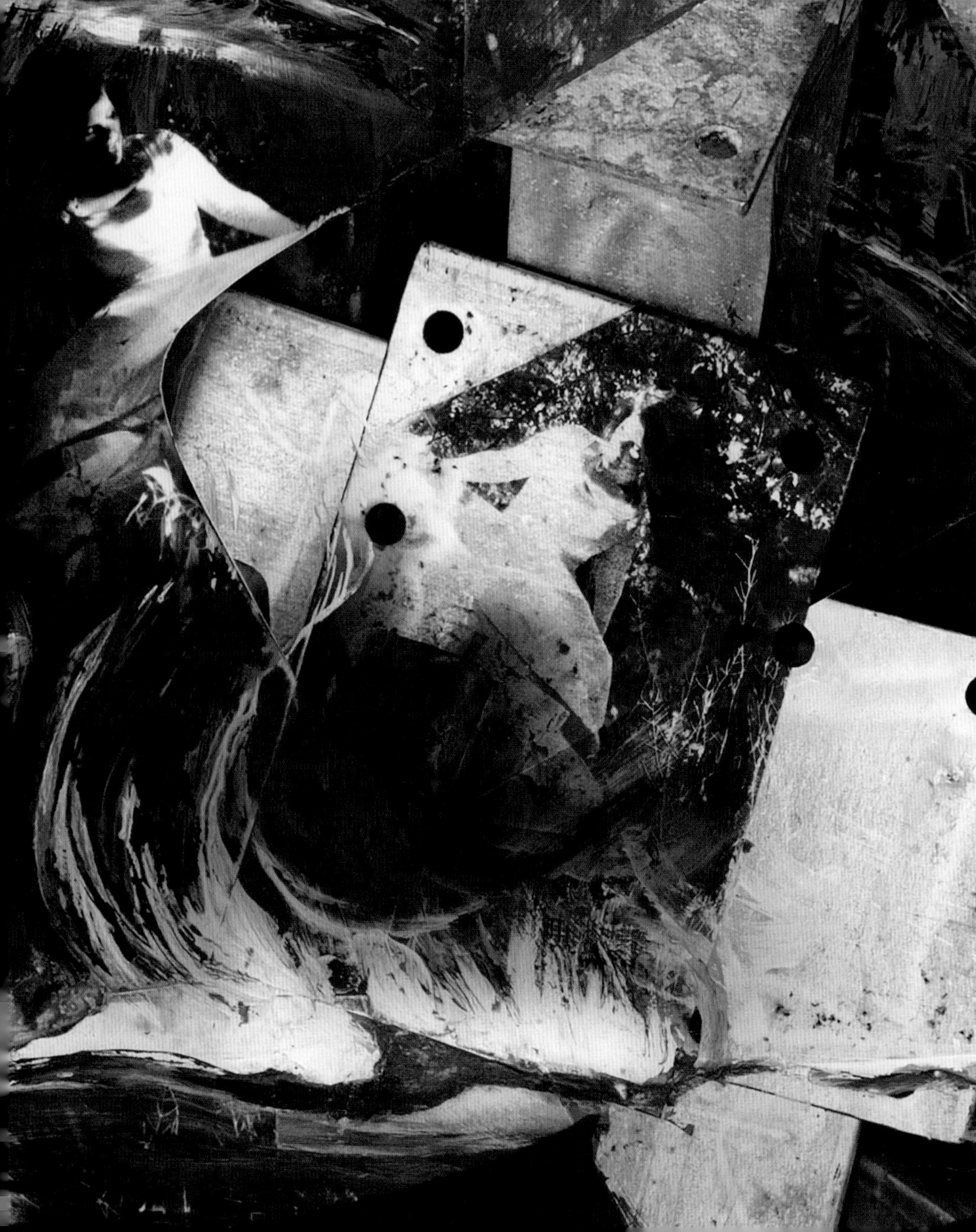

with smoke from the glory of God, and from His power; and no man was able to enter into the temple, till the seven plagues of the seven angels were fulfilled.

And I heard a great voice out of the temple saying to the seven angels, Go your ways, and pour out the vials of the wrath of God upon the earth.

And the first went, and poured out his vial upon the earth; and there fell a noisome and grievous sore upon the men which had the mark of the beast, and upon them which worshiped his image. And the second angel poured out his vial upon the sea; and it became as the blood of a dead man: and every living soul died in the sea. And the third angel poured out his vial upon the rivers and fountains of waters; and they became blood.

And I heard the angel of the waters say, You are righteous, O Lord, which are, and were, and shall be, because You have judged thus. For they have shed the blood of saints and prophets, and You have given them blood to drink; for they are worthy. And I heard another out of the altar say, Even so, Lord God Almighty, true and righteous are Your judgments.

And the fourth angel poured out his vial upon the sun; and power was given to him to scorch men with fire. And men were scorched with great heat, and blasphemed the name of God, which hath power over these plagues: and they repented not to give Him glory. And the fifth angel poured out his vial upon the seat of the beast; and his kingdom was full of darkness; and they gnawed their tongues for pain, and blasphemed the God of heaven because of their pains and their sores, and repented not of their deeds.

And the sixth angel poured out his vial upon the great river Euphrates; and the water thereof was dried up, that the way of the kings of the east might be prepared. And I saw three unclean spirits like frogs come out of the mouth of the dragon, and out of the mouth of the beast, and out of the mouth of the false prophet. For they are the spirits of devils, working miracles, which go forth to the kings of the earth and of the whole world, to gather them to the battle of that great day of God Almighty.

Behold, I come as a thief. Blessed is he that watches, and keeps his garments, lest he walk naked, and they see his shame. And he gathered them together into a place called in the Hebrew tongue Armageddon.

And the seventh angel poured out his vial into the air; and there came a great voice out of the temple of heaven, from the throne, saying, It is done.

And there were voices, and thunders, and lightnings; and there was a great earthquake, such as was not since men were upon the earth, so mighty an earthquake, and so great. And the great city was divided into three parts, and the cities of the nations fell: and great Babylon came in remembrance before God, to give to her the cup of the wine of the fierceness of His wrath. And every island fled away, and the mountains were not found.

And there fell upon men a great hail out of heaven, every stone about the weight of a talent: and men blasphemed God because of the plague of the hail; for the plague thereof was exceeding great.

ROOM 4

TRUE KNOWLEDGE OF SATAN

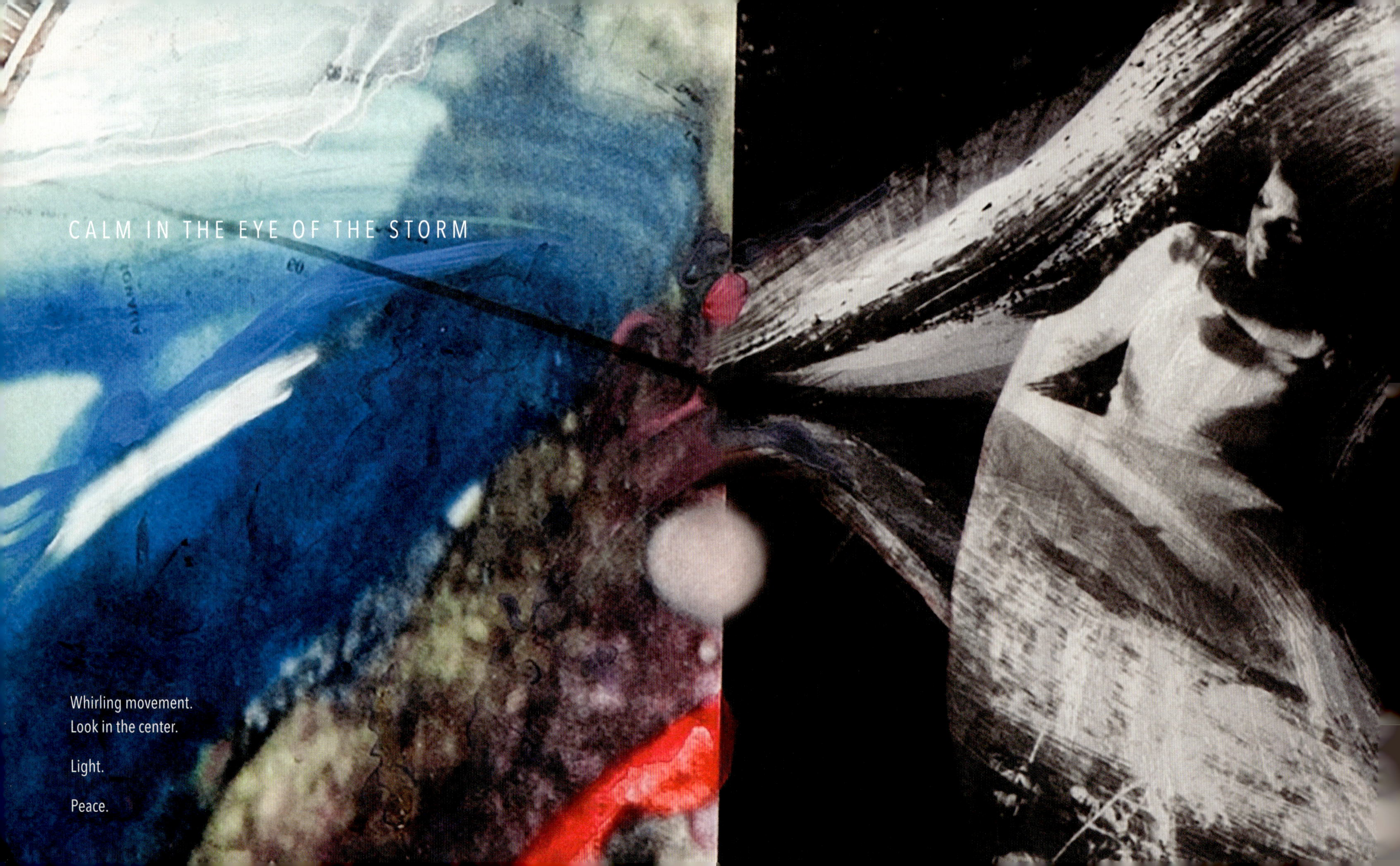
CALM IN THE EYE OF THE STORM

Whirling movement.
Look in the center.

Light.

Peace.

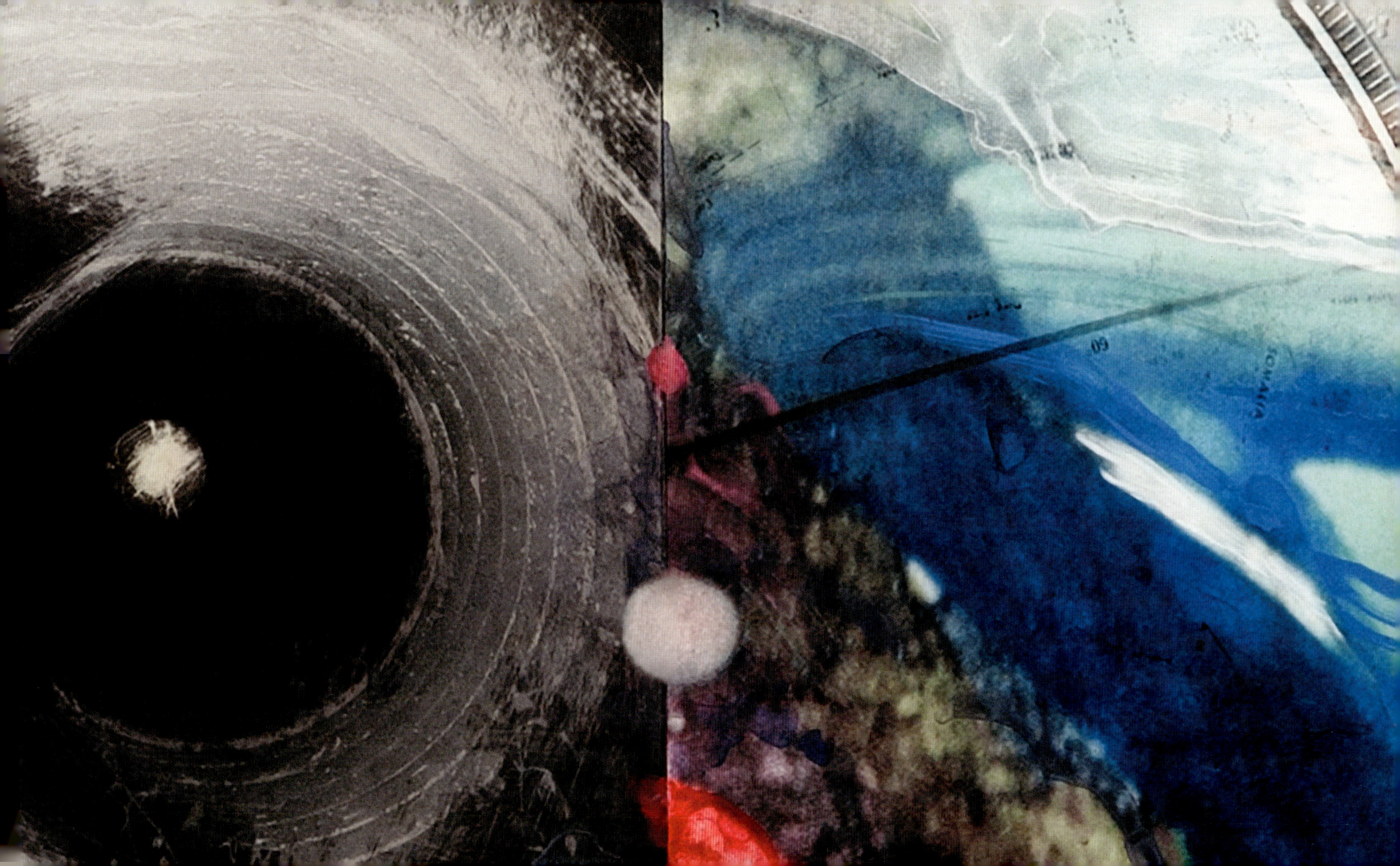

REFUGE

Destruction may surround, but God's peace provides refuge.

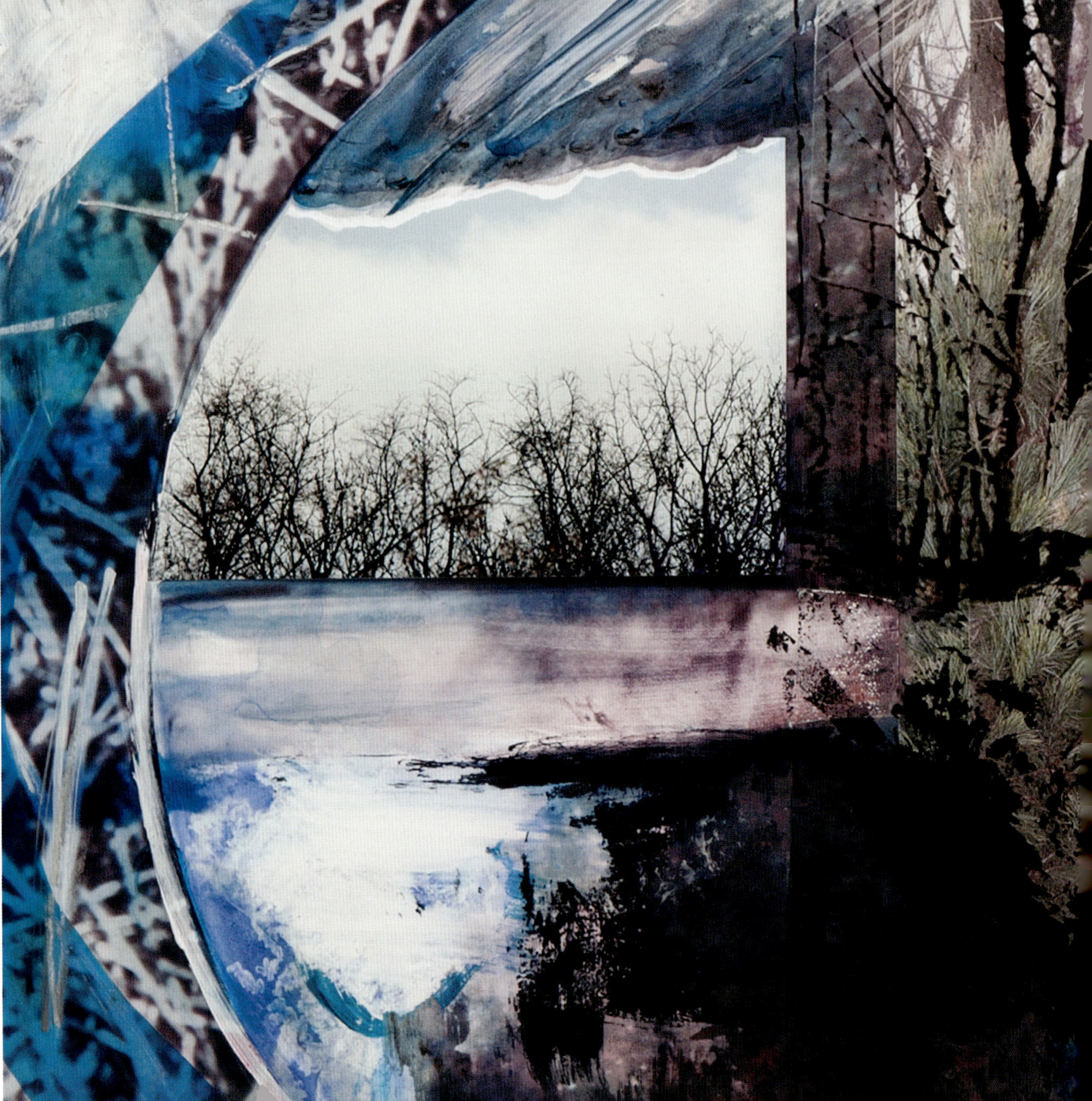

"Stand on the sea of glass" (Revelation 15:2).

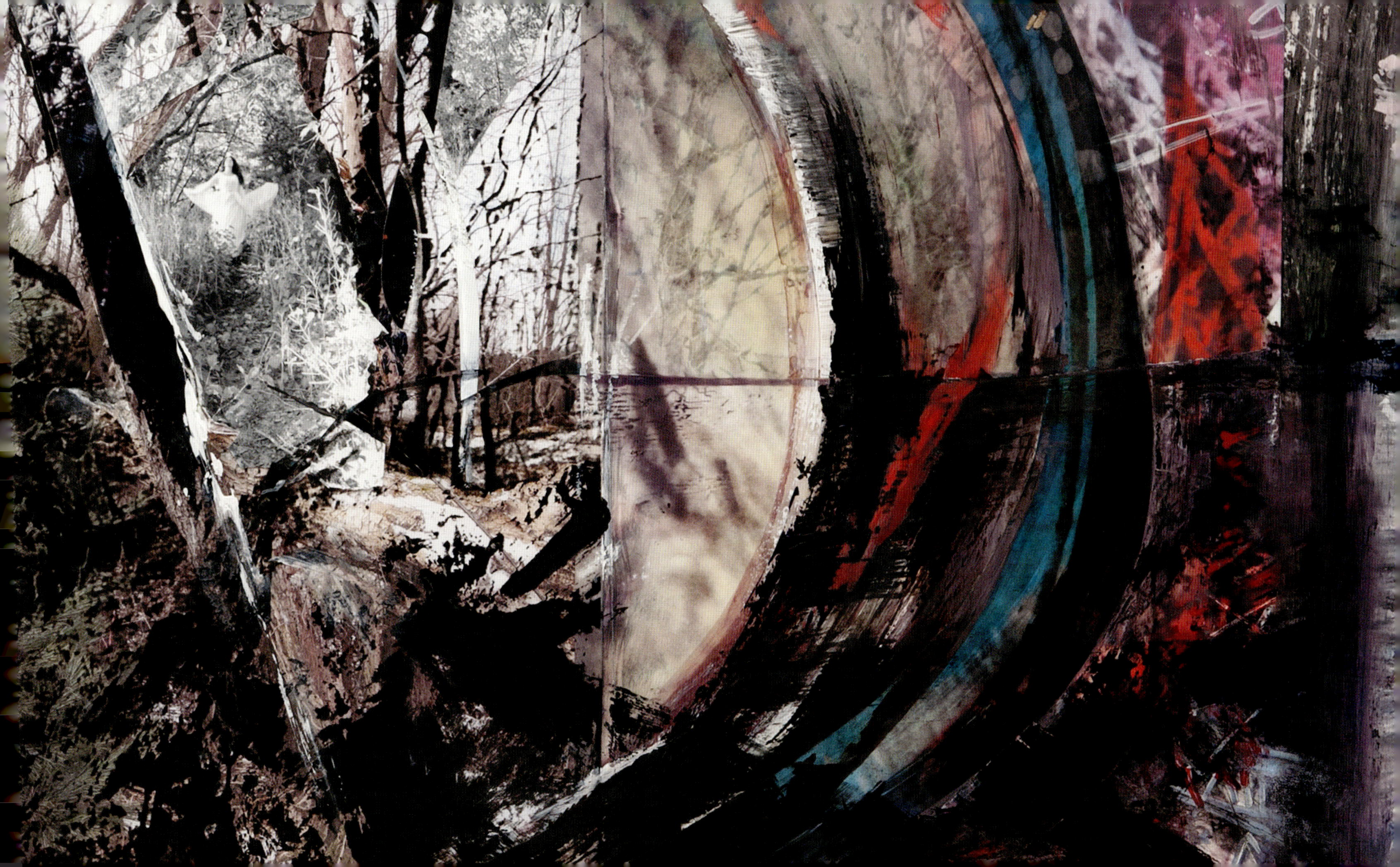

THROUGH A GLASS DARKLY

In times of confusion, keep your eyes on Him.

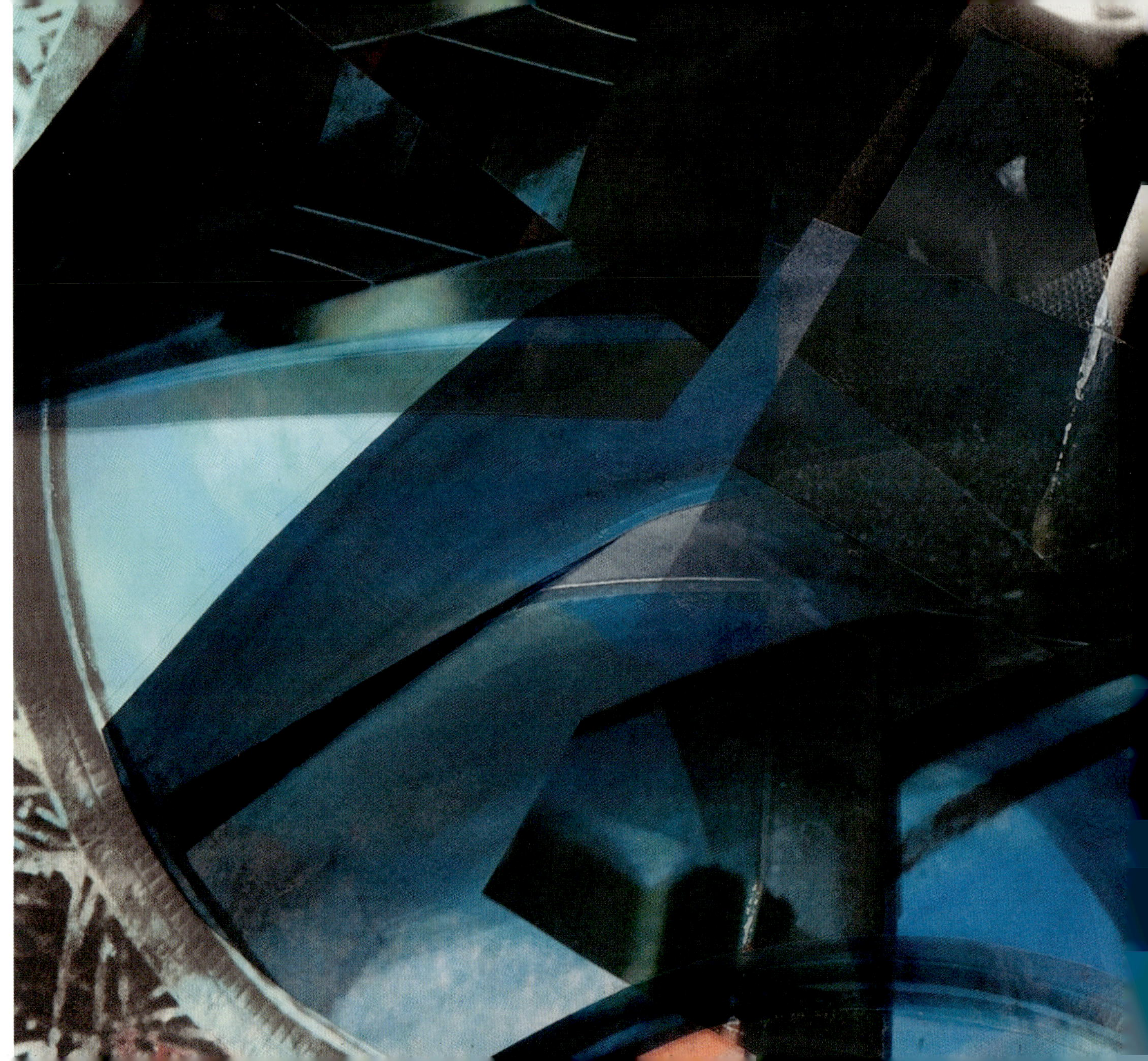

*"They overcame [Satan] by the blood of the Lamb,
and by the word of their testimony; and they
loved not their lives to the death"* (Revelation 12:11).

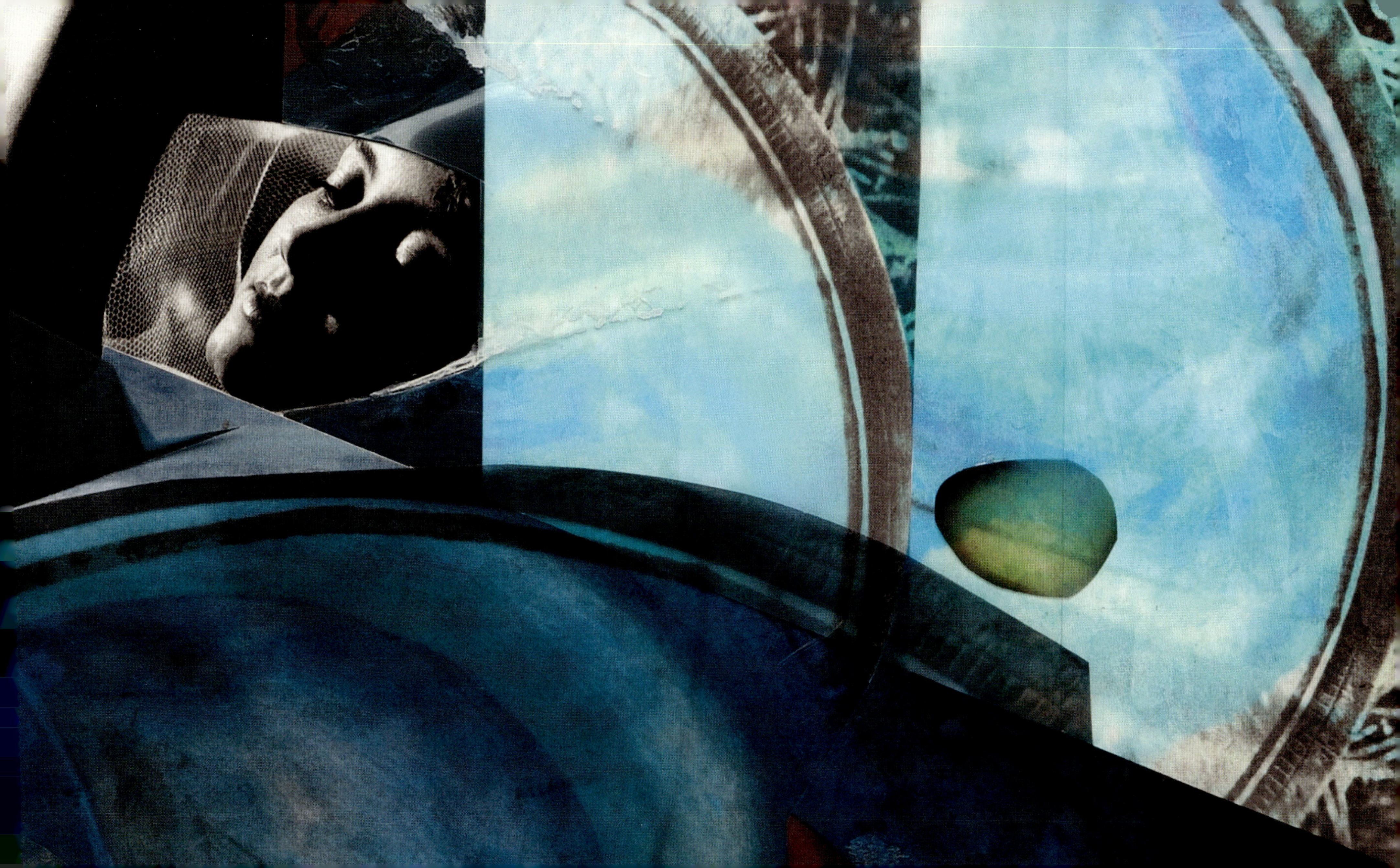

CATACLYSM

Everything that can be shaken will be shaken.

*"And there were voices, and thunders, and lightnings…
and every island fled away, and the mountains were not found"* (Revelation 16:18, 20).

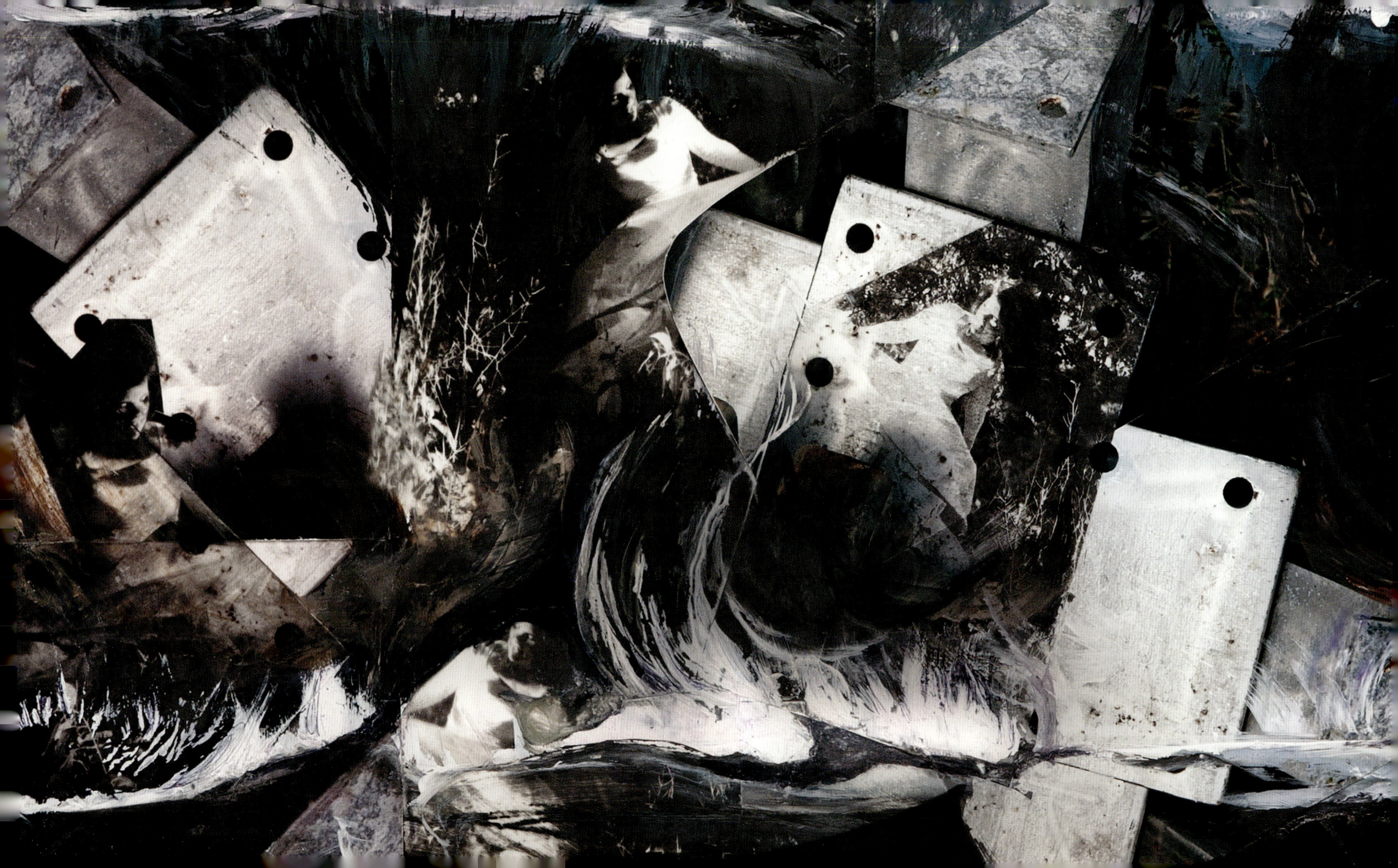

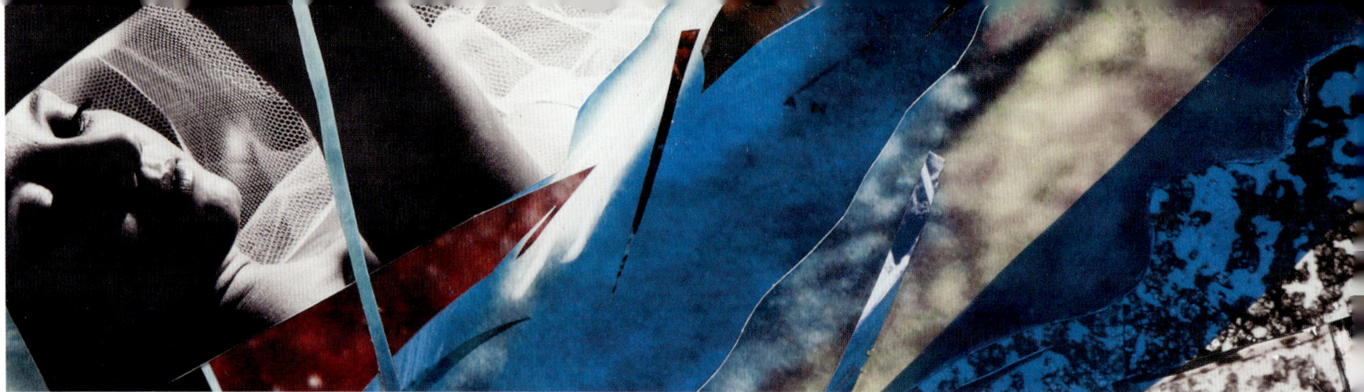

And there came one of the seven angels which had the seven vials, and talked with me, saying unto me, Come hither; I will show to you the judgment of the great whore that sits upon many waters: with whom the kings of the earth have committed fornication, and the inhabitants of the earth have been made drunk with the wine of her fornication.

So he carried me away in the Spirit into the wilderness: and I saw a woman sit upon a scarlet colored beast, full of names of blasphemy, having seven heads and ten horns. And the woman was arrayed in purple and scarlet color, and decked with gold and precious stones and pearls, having a golden cup in her hand full of abominations and filthiness of her fornication: and upon her forehead was a name written, MYSTERY, BABYLON THE GREAT, THE MOTHER OF HARLOTS AND ABOMINATIONS OF THE EARTH.

And I saw the woman drunken with the blood of the saints, and with the blood of the martyrs of Jesus: and when I saw her, I wondered with great admiration. And the angel said to me, Wherefore did you marvel? I will tell you the mystery of the woman, and of the beast that carries her, which has the seven heads and ten horns. The beast that you saw was, and is not; and shall ascend out of the bottomless pit, and go into perdition: and they that dwell on the earth shall wonder, whose names were not written in the book of life from the foundation of the world, when they behold the beast that was, and is not, and yet is.

And here is the mind which has wisdom. The seven heads are seven mountains, on which the woman sits. And there are seven kings: five are fallen, and one is, and the other is not yet come; and when he comes, he must continue a short space.

And the beast that was, and is not, even he is the eighth, and is of the seven, and goes into perdition. And the ten horns which you saw are ten kings, which have received no kingdom as yet; but receive power as kings one hour with the beast. These have one mind, and shall give their power and strength to the beast. These shall make war with the Lamb, and the Lamb shall overcome them: for He is Lord of lords, and King of kings: and they that are with Him are called, and chosen, and faithful.

And he says unto me, The waters which you saw, where the whore sits, are peoples, and multitudes, and nations, and tongues. And the ten horns which you saw upon the beast, these shall hate the whore, and shall make her desolate and naked, and shall eat her flesh, and burn her with fire. For God has put in their hearts to fulfill His will, and to agree, and give their kingdom to the beast, until the words of God shall be fulfilled. And the woman which you saw is that great city, which reigns over the kings of the earth.

And after these things I saw another angel come down from heaven, having great power; and the earth was lightened with his glory. And he cried mightily with a strong voice, saying, Babylon the great is fallen, is fallen, and is become the habitation of devils, and the hold of every foul spirit, and a cage of every unclean and hateful bird. For all nations have drunk of the wine of the wrath of her fornication, and the kings of the earth have committed fornication with her, and the merchants of the earth are waxed rich through the abundance of her delicacies.

And I heard another voice from heaven, saying, Come out of her, my people, that you be not partakers of her sins, and that you receive not of her plagues. For her sins have reached to heaven, and God has remembered her iniquities. Reward her even as she rewarded you, and double to her double according to her works: in the cup which she has filled fill to her double. How much she has glorified herself, and lived deliciously, so much torment and sorrow give her: for she says in her heart, I sit a queen, and am no widow, and shall see no sorrow.

Therefore shall her plagues come in one day, death, and mourning, and famine; and she shall be utterly burned with fire: for strong is the Lord God who judges her. And the kings of the earth, who have committed fornication and lived deliciously with her, shall bewail her, and lament for her, when they shall see the smoke of her burning, standing afar off for the fear of her torment, saying, Alas, alas, that great city Babylon, that mighty city! for in one hour is your judgment come.

And the merchants of the earth shall weep and mourn over her; for no man buys their merchandise any more: The merchandise of gold, and silver, and precious stones, and of pearls, and fine linen, and purple, and silk, and scarlet, and all thyine wood, and all manner vessels of ivory, and all manner vessels of most precious wood, and of brass, and iron, and marble, and cinnamon, and odors, and ointments, and frankincense, and wine, and oil, and fine flour, and wheat, and beasts, and sheep, and horses, and chariots, and slaves, and souls of men. And the fruits that your soul lusted after are departed from you, and all things which were dainty and goodly are departed from you, and you shalt find them no more at all.

The merchants of these things, which were made rich by her, shall stand afar off for the fear of her torment, weeping and wailing, and saying, Alas, alas, that great city, that was clothed in fine linen, and purple, and scarlet, and decked with gold, and precious stones, and pearls! For in one hour so great riches is come to nothing. And every shipmaster, and all the company in ships, and sailors, and as many as trade by sea, stood afar off, and cried when they saw the smoke of her burning, saying, What city is like to this great city!

And they cast dust on their heads, and cried, weeping and wailing, saying, Alas, alas, that great city, wherein were made rich all that had ships in the sea by reason of her costliness! for in one hour is she made desolate.

Rejoice over her, you heaven, and you holy apostles and prophets; for God has avenged you on her. And a mighty angel took up a stone like a great millstone, and cast it into the sea, saying, Thus with violence shall that great city Babylon be thrown down, and shall be found no more at all.

And the voice of harpers, and musicians, and of pipers, and trumpeters, shall be heard no more at all in you; and no craftsman, of whatsoever craft he be, shall be found any more in you; and the sound of a millstone shall be heard no more at all in you; and the light of a candle shall shine no more at all in you; and the voice of the bridegroom and of the bride shall be heard no more at all in you: for your merchants were the great men of the earth; for by your sorceries were all nations deceived.

And in her was found the blood of prophets, and of saints, and of all that were slain upon the earth.

ROOM 5

THE FALL OF SATAN'S DECEPTIONS

SATAN'S PROSPERITY

THE FIGURE IS BURIED IN TRANSPARENCY TO CREATE THE ILLUSION OF BEING ENGULFED IN FLAMES.

Within the world is sprung up a false church; a church whose ruler is Satan.

"Drunken with the blood of the saints,
and with the blood of the martyrs of Jesus" (Revelation 17:6).

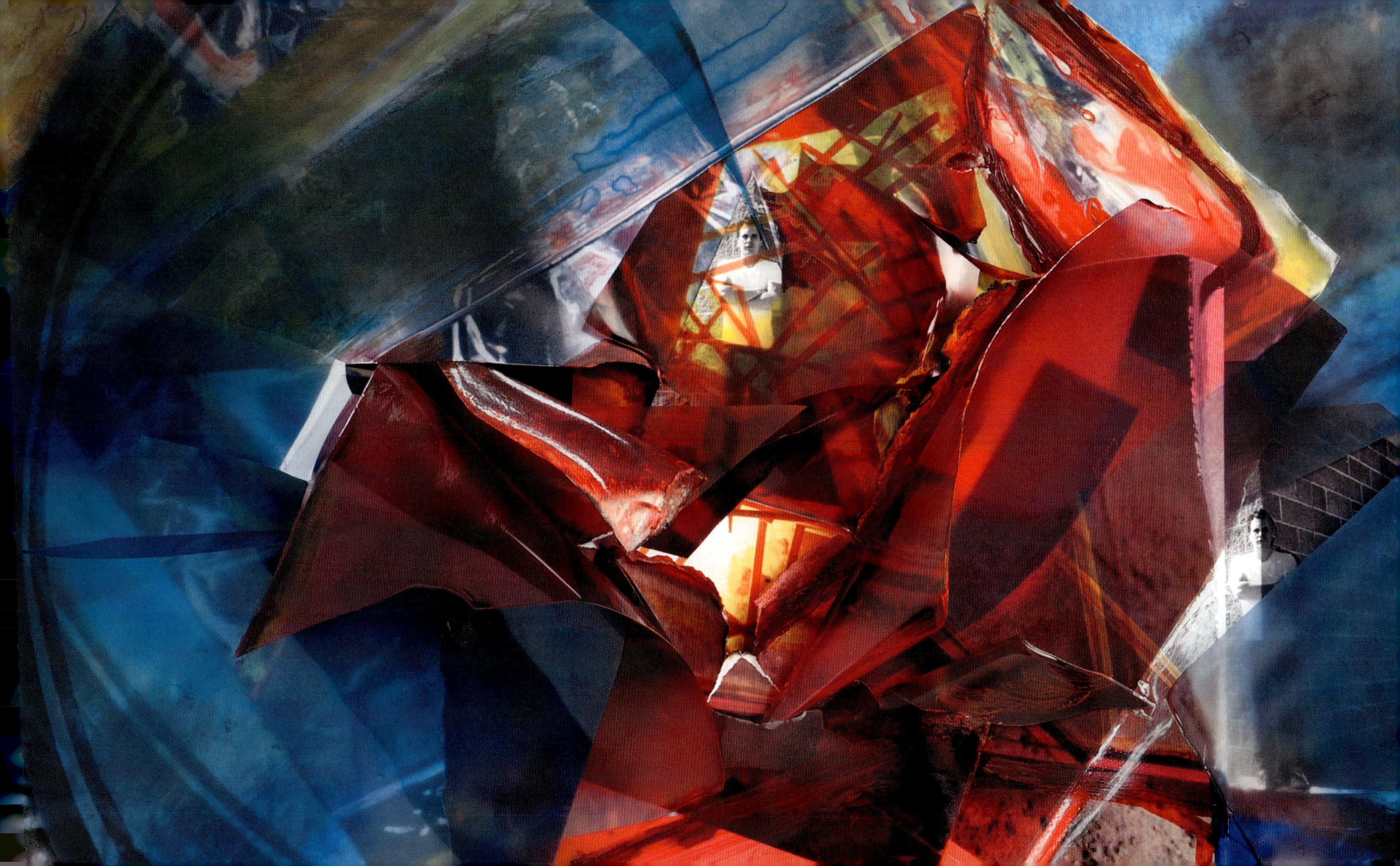

NOT THE TIME

This is not the time to be undecided.

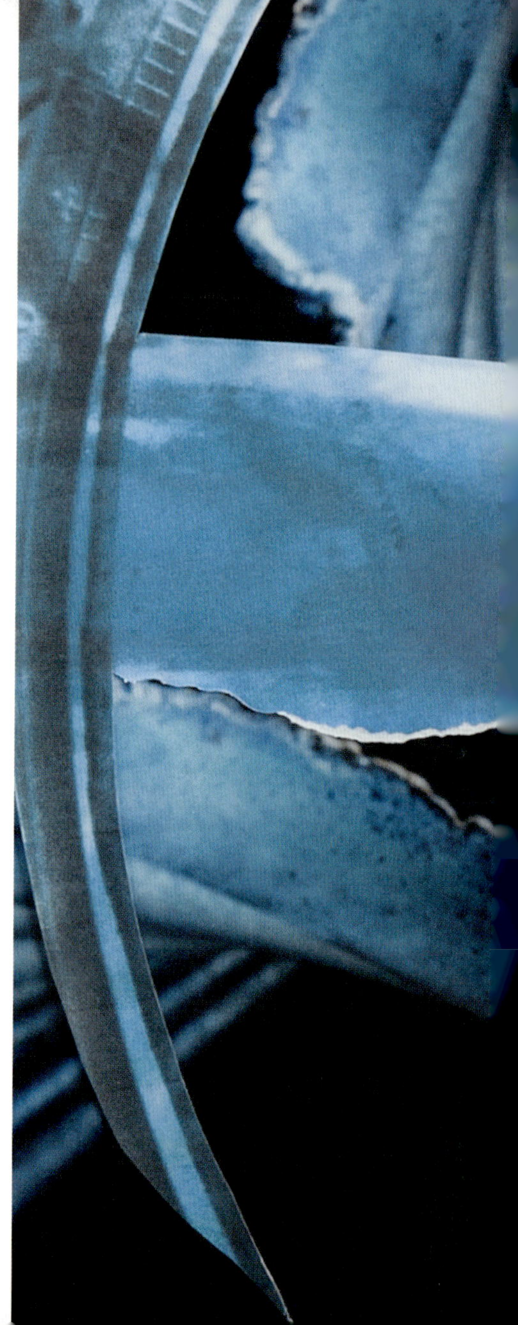

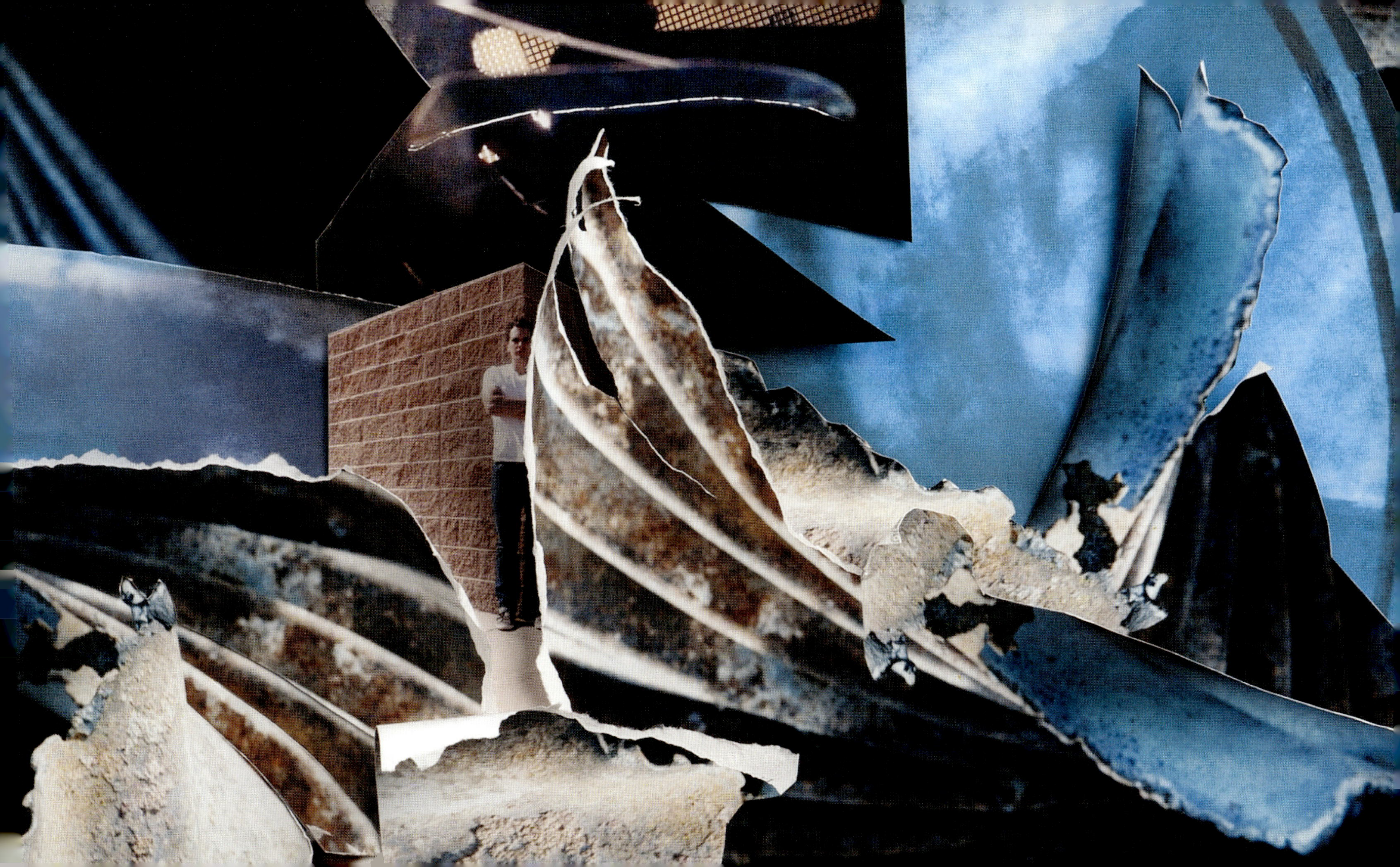

ARISE, O SLEEPER

This is not the time to be asleep.

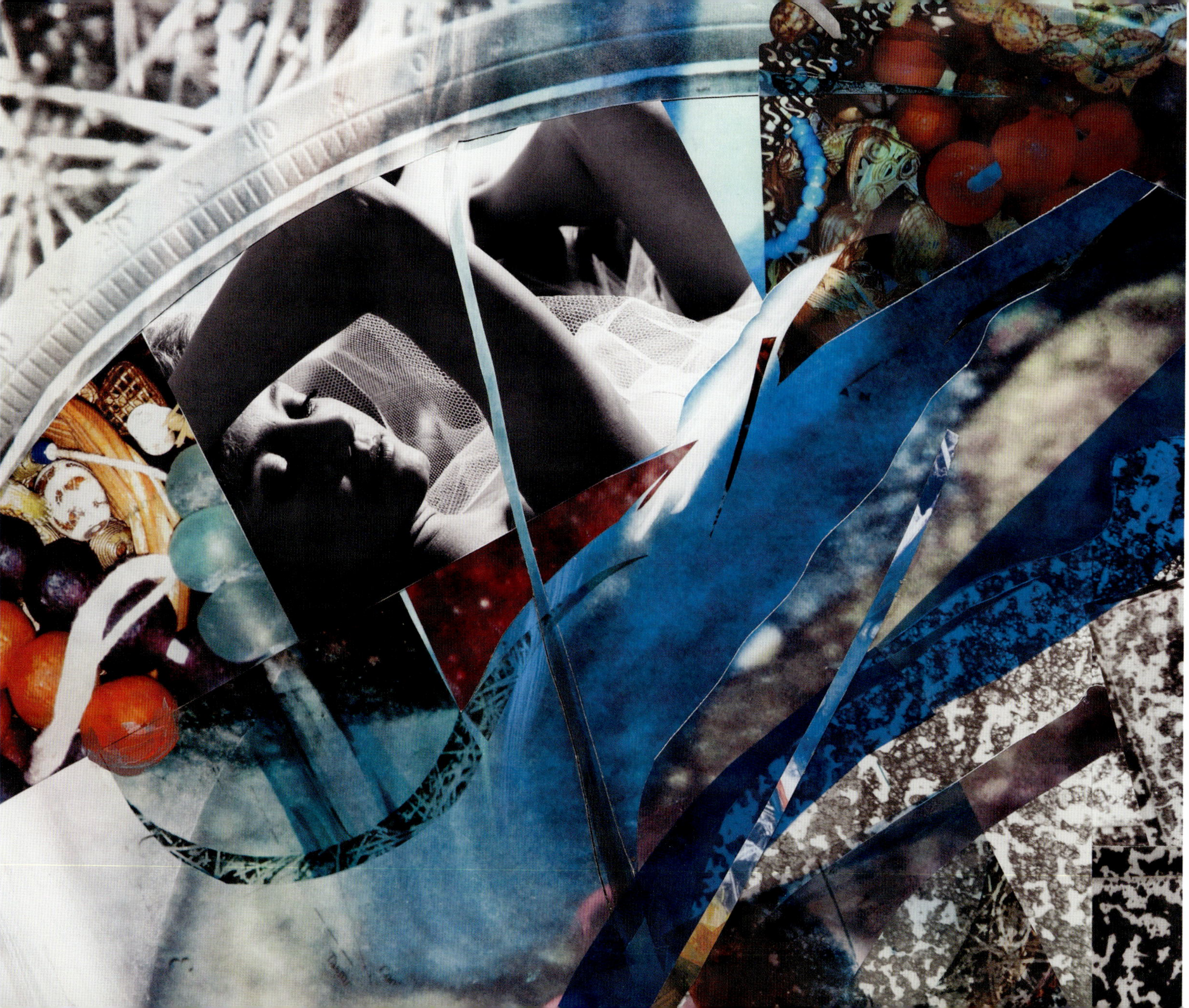

This is a time when people hide themselves.

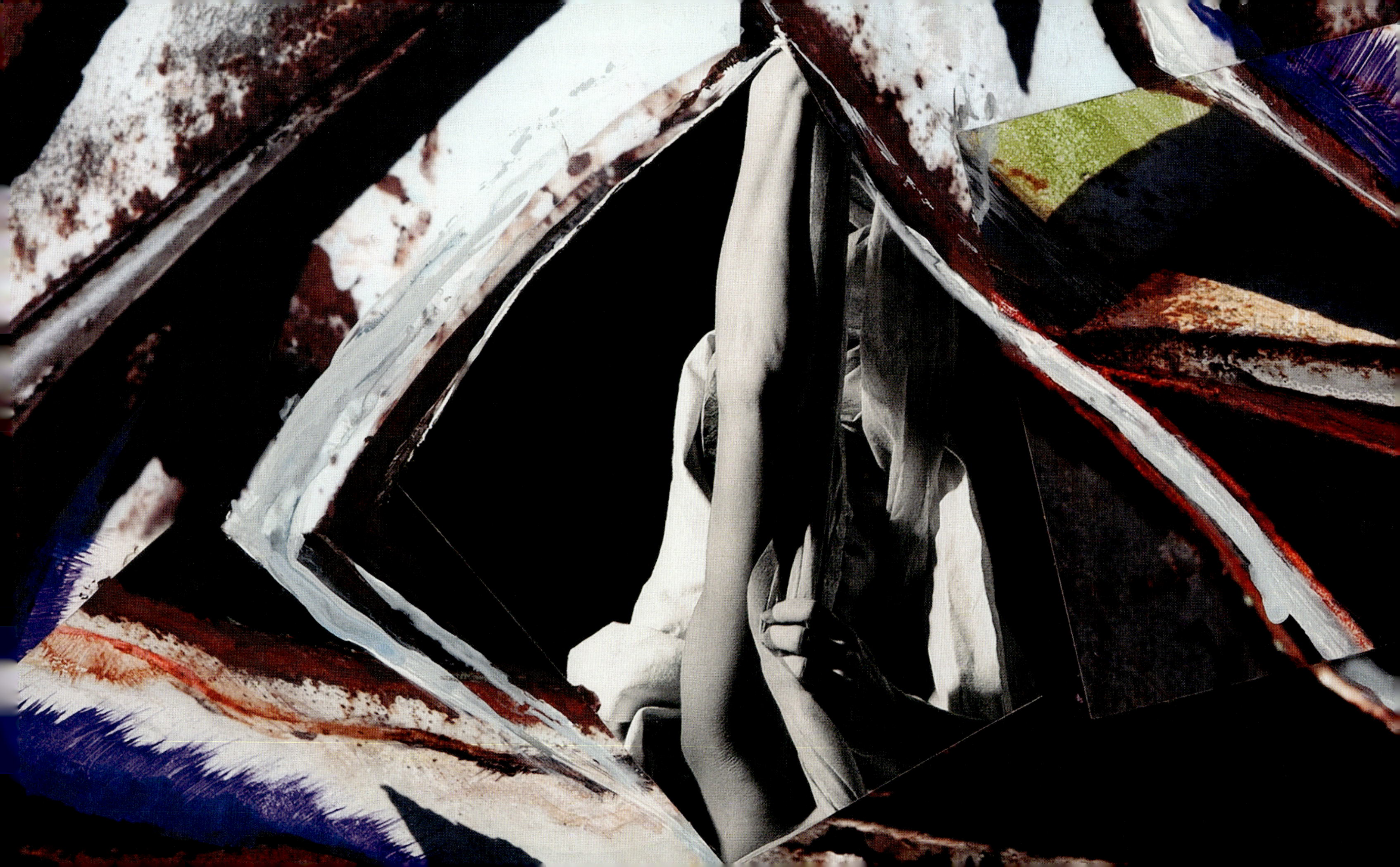

DESCENT

But who can hide from God?

"Weep and mourn over her" (Revelation 18:11).

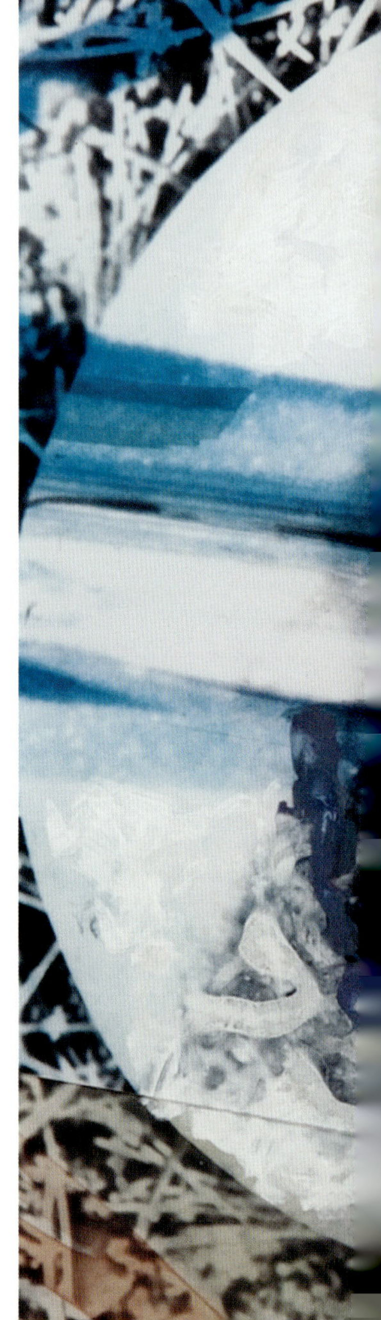

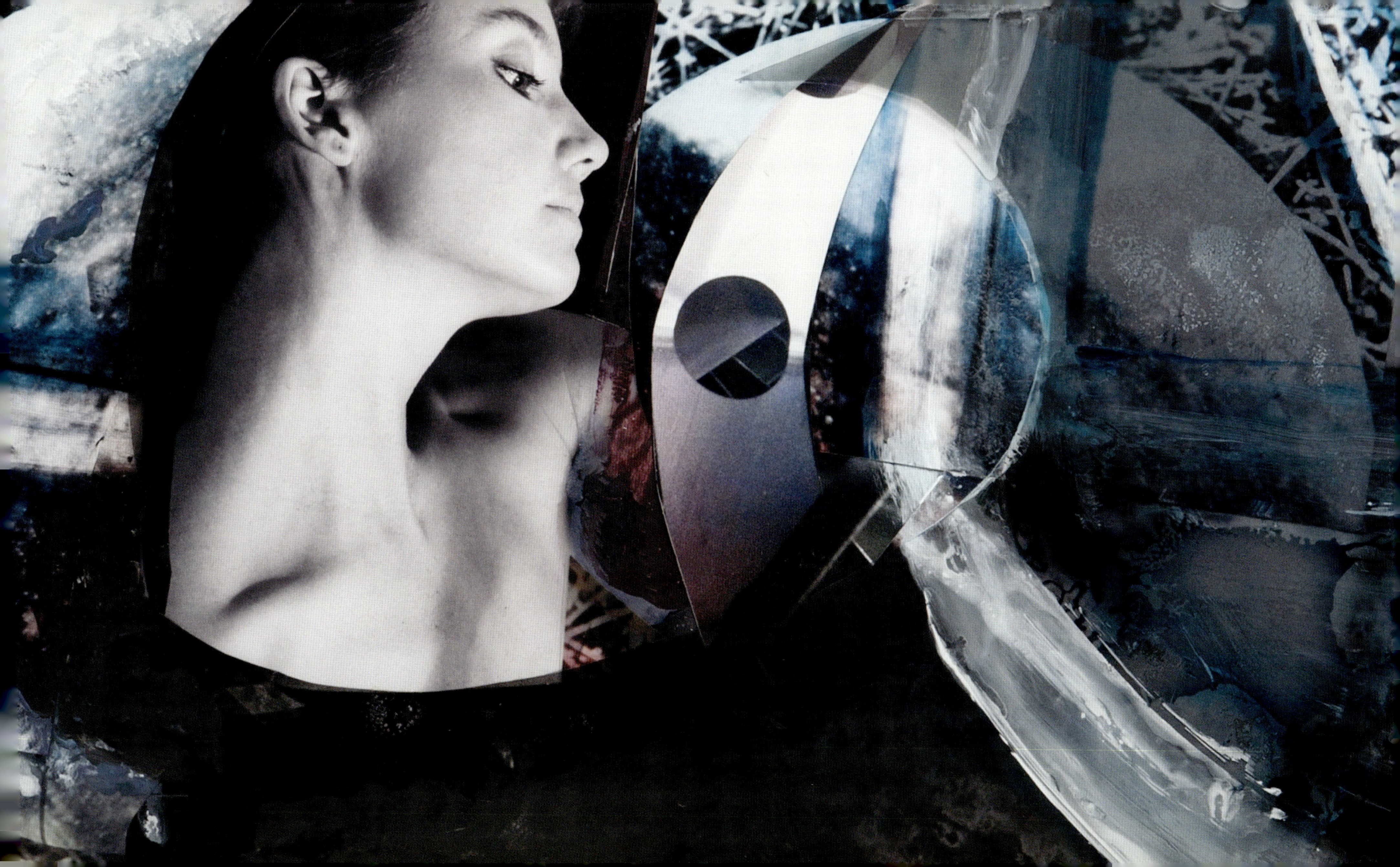

REND APART

A glimpse of Satan's rule.

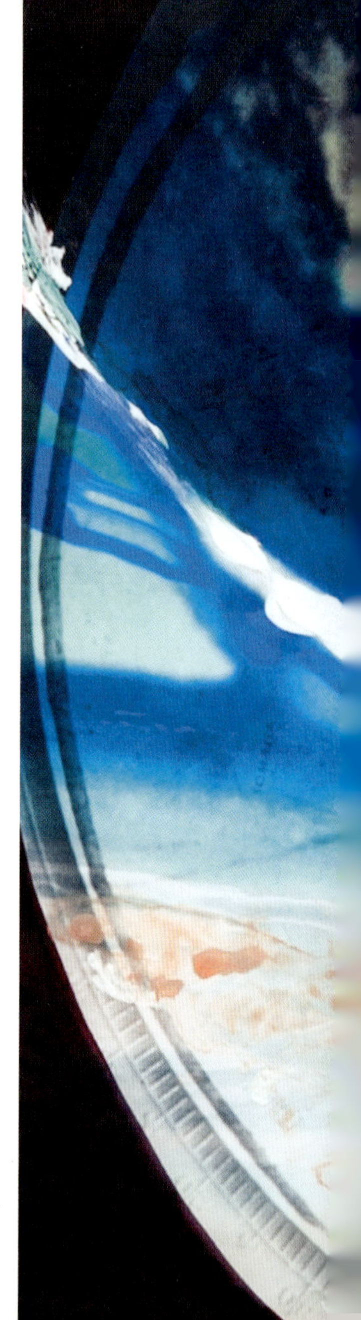

"Alas, alas, that great city Babylon" (Revelation 18:10).

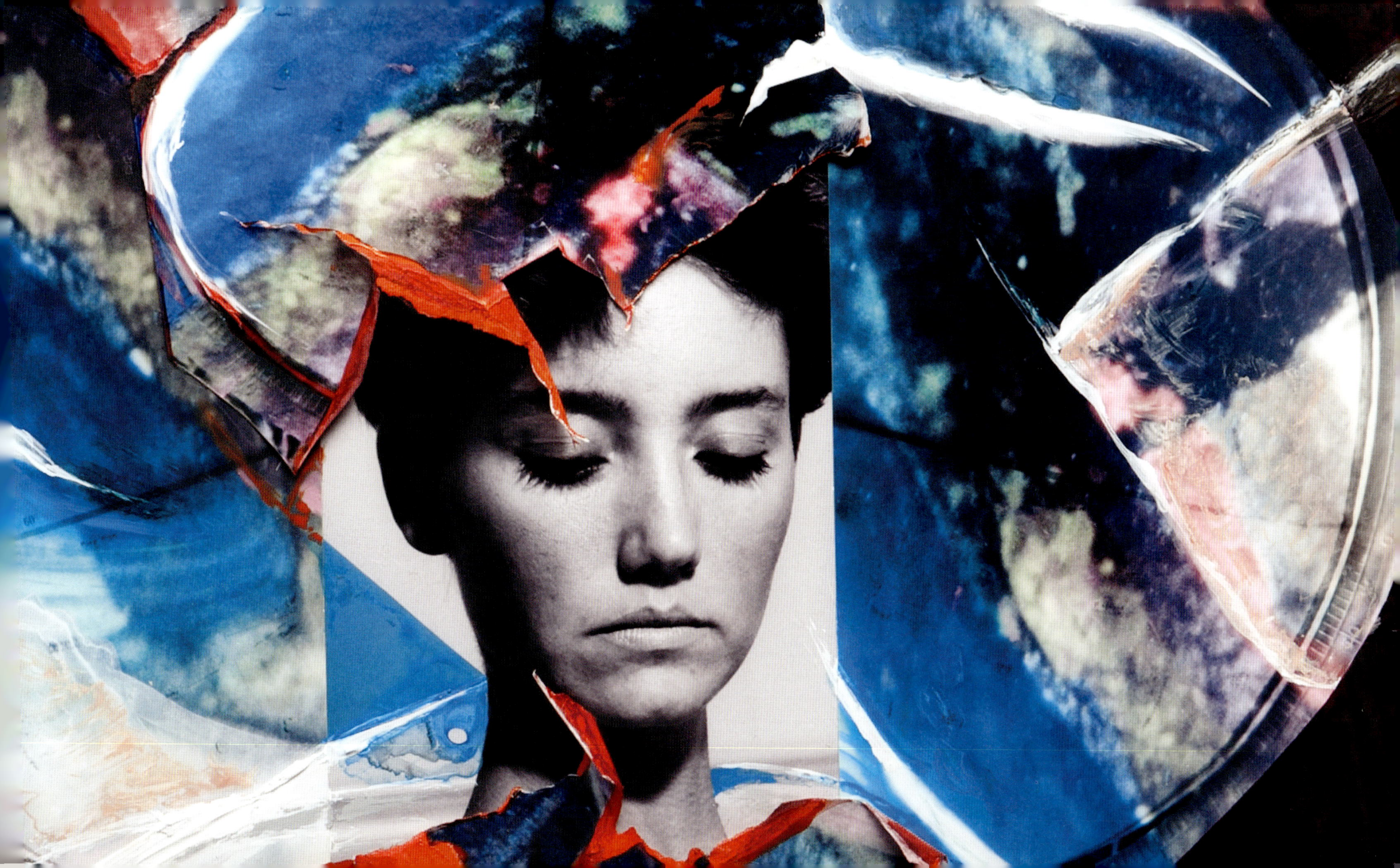

BREAKING POINT

THE METAL SIGNIFIES THE STATE OF ONE UNDER SATAN'S RULE.
THE FIGURE IS FRAGMENTED, THE BROKEN STATE OF ONE WHO LIVES
OUTSIDE OF WHAT THEY ARE CALLED TO BE DOING.

Satan wants to break everyone.

"And the voice of harpers, and musicians, and of pipers, and trumpeters, shall be heard no more at all in you; and no craftsman, of whatsoever craft he be, shall be found any more in you; and the sound of a millstone shall be heard no more at all in you; and the light of a candle shall shine no more at all in you; and the voice of the bridegroom and of the bride shall be heard no more at all in you" (Revelation 18:22–23).

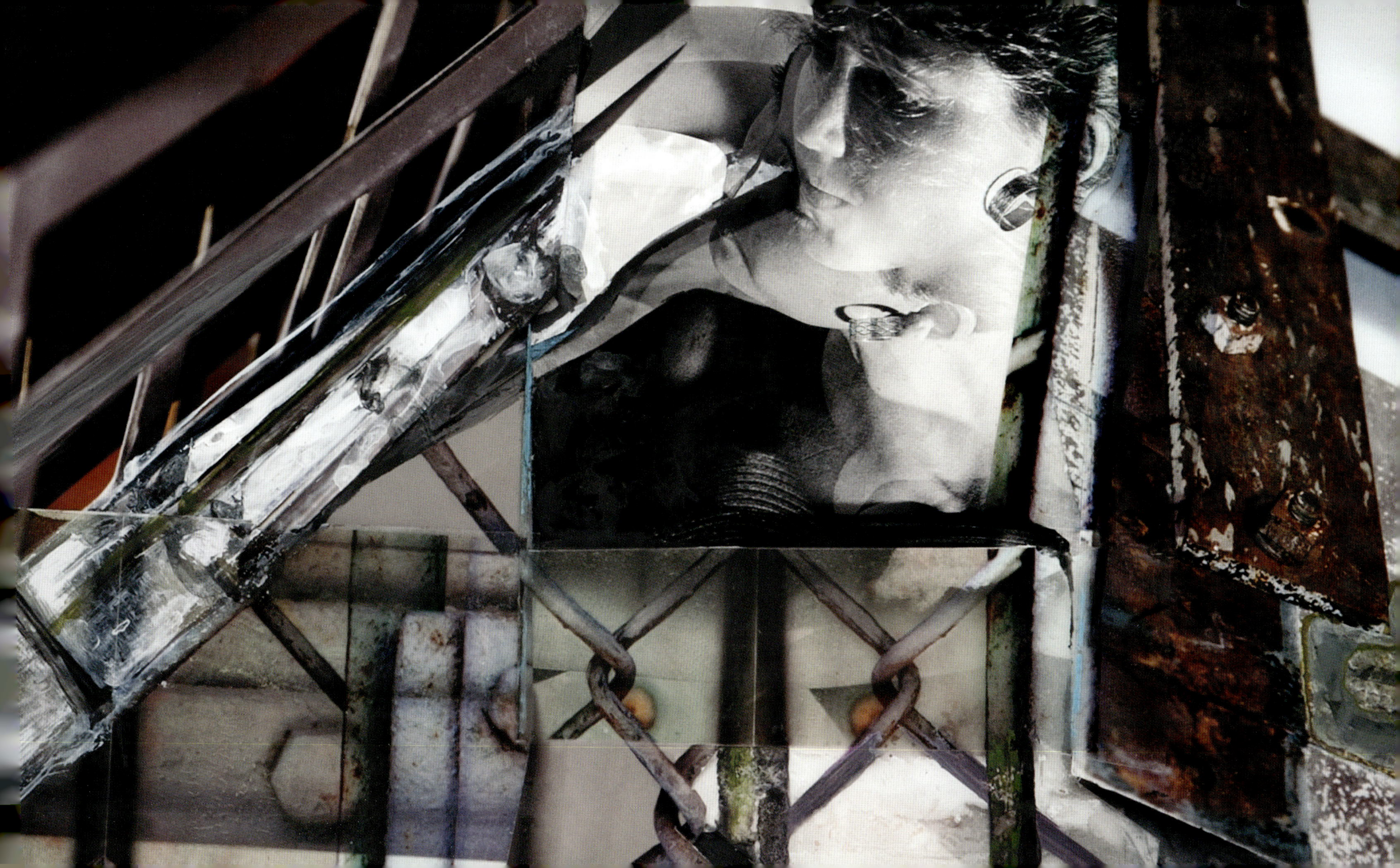

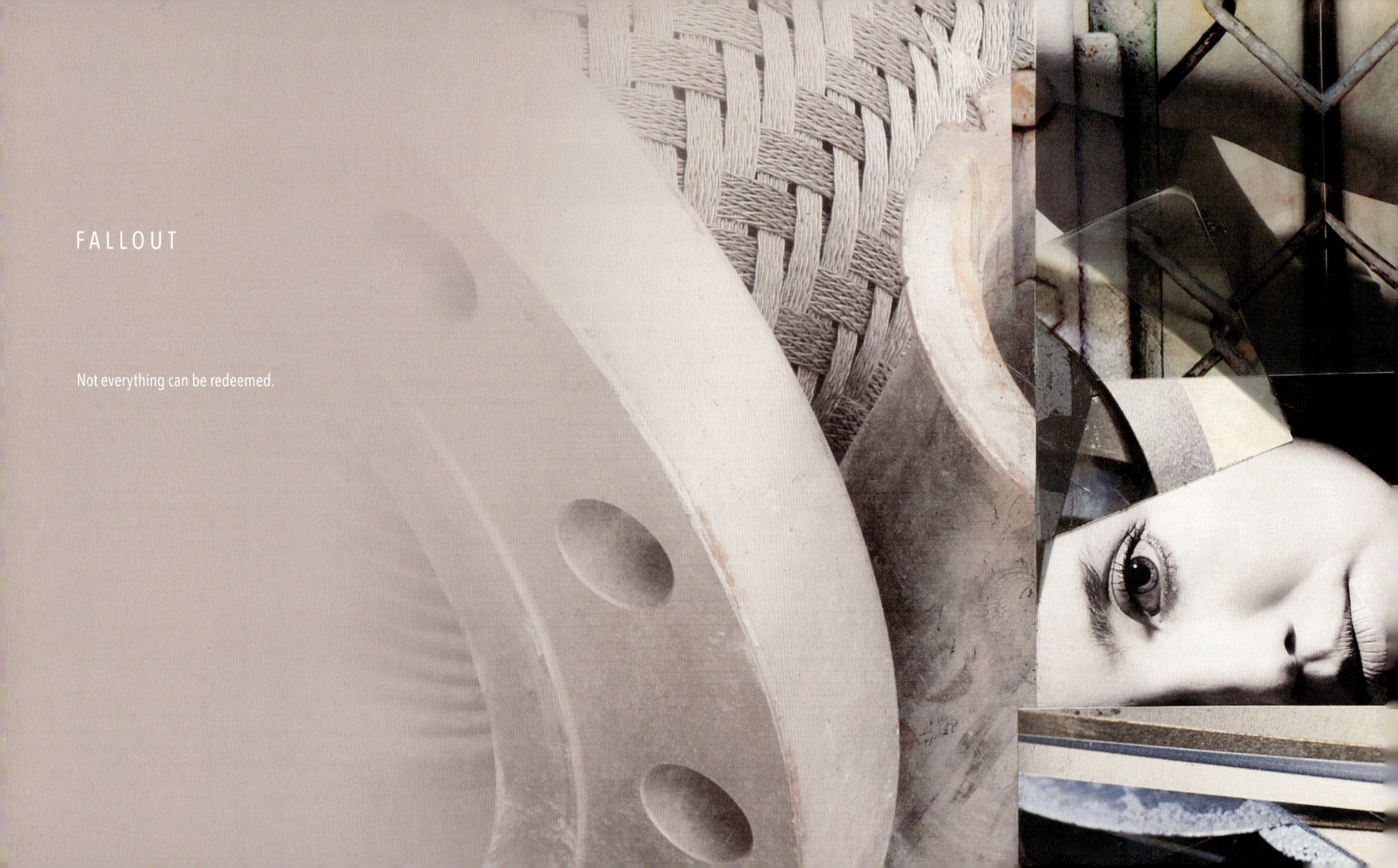
FALLOUT
Not everything can be redeemed.

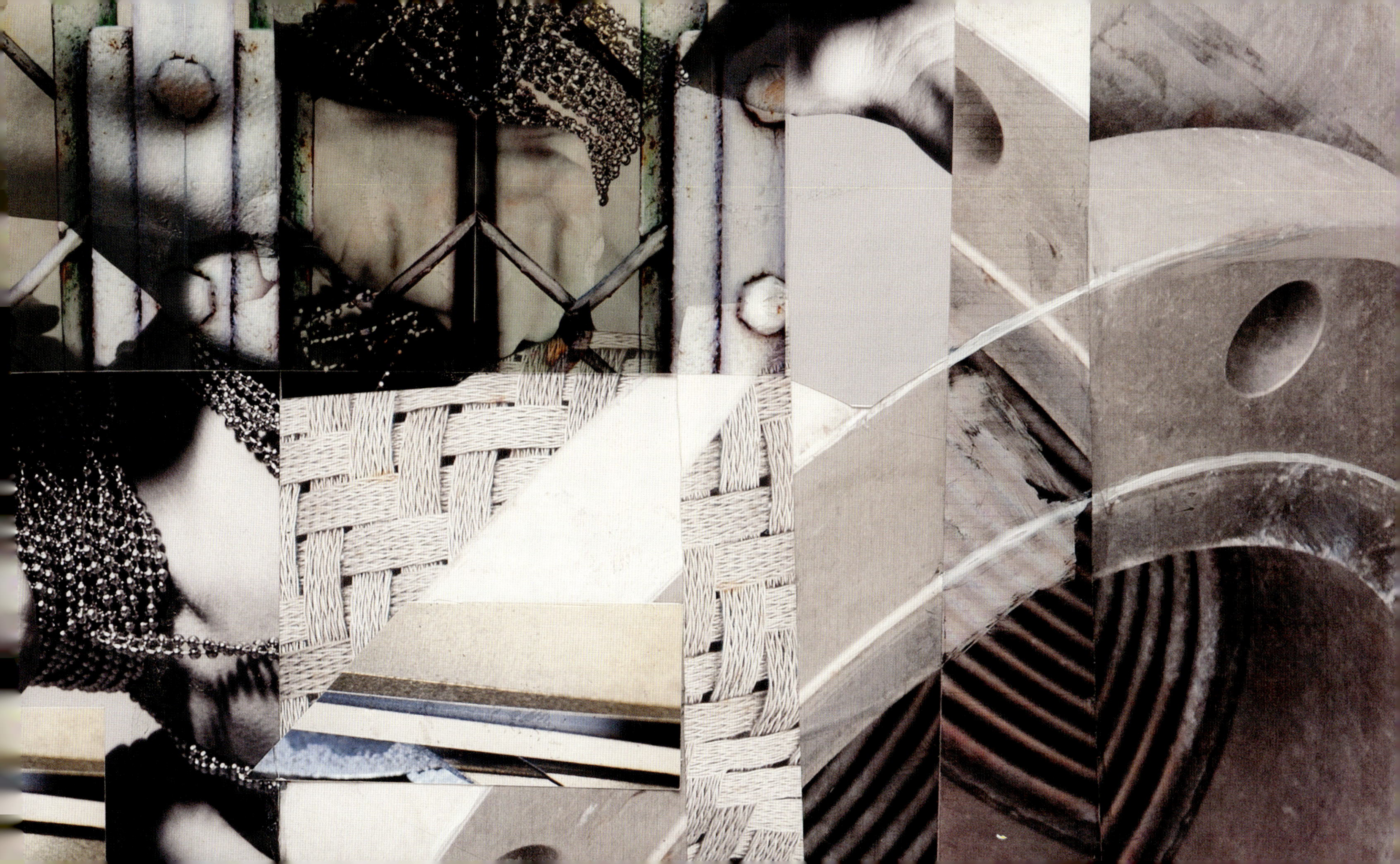

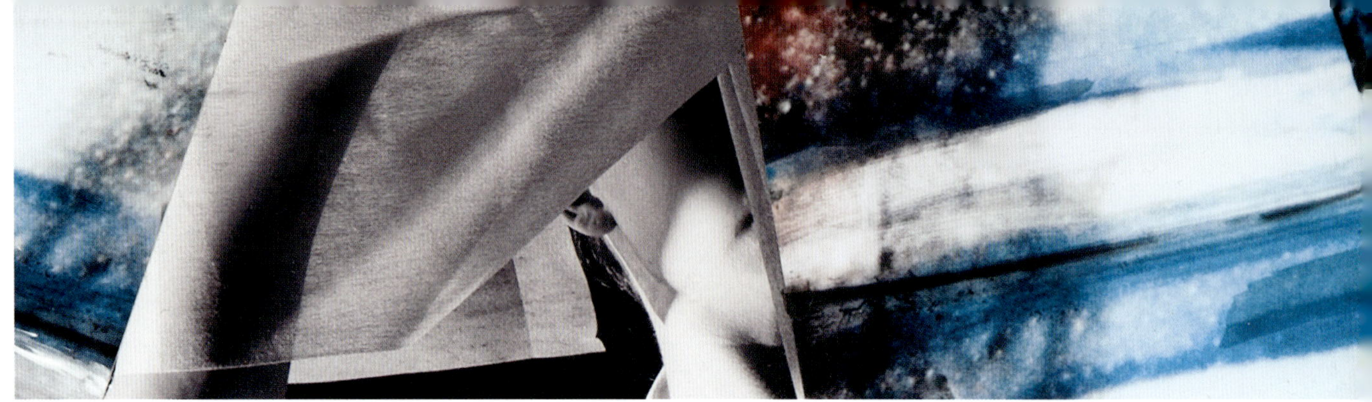

19-20

And after these things I heard a great voice of much people in heaven, saying, Alleluia; salvation, and glory, and honor, and power, to the Lord our God: for true and righteous are His judgments: for He has judged the great whore, which did corrupt the earth with her fornication, and has avenged the blood of His servants at her hand.

And again they said, Alleluia. And her smoke rose up for ever and ever. And the four and twenty elders and the four beasts fell down and worshiped God that sat on the throne, saying, Amen; Alleluia.

And a voice came out of the throne, saying, Praise our God, all you His servants, and you that fear Him, both small and great. And I heard as it were the voice of a great multitude, and as the voice of many waters, and as the voice of mighty thunderings, saying, Alleluia: for the Lord God omnipotent reigns. Let us be glad and rejoice, and give honor to Him: for the marriage of the Lamb is come, and His wife has made herself ready. And to her was granted that she should be arrayed in fine linen, clean and white: for the fine linen is the righteousness of saints.

And he says to me, Write, Blessed are they which are called unto the marriage supper of the Lamb. And he says to me, These are the true sayings of God. And I fell at his feet to worship him. And he said to me, See you do it not: I am your fellow-servant, and of your brethren that have the testimony of Jesus: worship God: for the testimony of Jesus is the spirit of prophecy.

And I saw heaven opened, and behold a white horse; and He that sat upon him was called Faithful and True, and in righteousness He does judge and make war. His eyes were as a flame of fire, and on His head were many crowns; and He had a name written, that no man knew, but He Himself. And He was clothed with a vesture dipped in blood: and His name is called The Word of God.

And the armies which were in heaven followed Him upon white horses, clothed in fine linen, white and clean. And out of His mouth goes a sharp sword, that with it He should smite the nations: and He shall rule them with a rod of iron: and He treads the winepress of the fierceness and wrath of Almighty God. And He has on His vesture and on His thigh a name written, KINGS OF KINGS AND LORD OF LORDS.

And I saw an angel standing in the sun; and he cried with a loud voice, saying to all the fowls that fly in the midst of heaven, Come and gather yourselves together to the supper of the great God; that you may eat the flesh of kings, and the flesh of captains, and the flesh of mighty men, and the flesh of horses, and of them that sit on them, and the flesh of all men, both free and bond, both small and great.

And I saw the beast, and the kings of the earth, and their armies, gathered together to make war against Him that sat on the horse, and against His army. And the beast was taken, and with him the false prophet that wrought miracles before him, with which he deceived them that had received the mark of the beast, and them that worshiped his image. These both were cast alive into a lake of fire burning with brimstone.

And the remnant were slain with the sword of Him that sat upon the horse, which sword proceeded out of His mouth: and all the fowls were filled with their flesh. And I saw an angel come down from heaven, having the key of the bottomless pit and a great chain in his hand.

And he laid hold on the dragon, that old serpent, which is the Devil, and Satan, and bound him a thousand years, and cast him into the bottomless pit, and shut him up, and set a seal upon him, that he should deceive the nations no more, till the thousand years should be fulfilled: and after that he must be loosed a little season.

And I saw thrones, and they sat upon them, and judgment was given to them: and I saw the souls of them that were beheaded for the witness of Jesus, and for the word of God, and which had not worshiped the beast, neither his image, neither had received his mark upon their foreheads, or in their hands; and they lived and reigned with Christ a thousand years.

But the rest of the dead lived not again until the thousand years were finished. This is the first resurrection. Blessed and holy is he that has part in the first resurrection: on such the second death has no power, but they shall be priests of God and of Christ, and shall reign with Him a thousand years. And when the thousand years are expired, Satan shall be loosed out of his prison, and shall go out to deceive the nations which are in the four quarters of the earth, Gog and Magog, to gather them together to battle: the number of whom is as the sand of the sea.

And they went up on the breadth of the earth, and compassed the camp of the saints about, and the beloved city: and fire came down from God out of heaven, and devoured them. And the devil that deceived them was cast into the lake of fire and brimstone, where the beast and the false prophet are, and shall be tormented day and night for ever and ever. And I saw a great white throne, and Him that sat on it, from whose face the earth and the heaven fled away; and there was found no place for them.

And I saw the dead, small and great, stand before God; and the books were opened: and another book was opened, which is the book of life: and the dead were judged out of those things which were written in the books according to their works. And the sea gave up the dead which were in it; and death and hell delivered up the dead which were in them: and they were judged every man according to their works. And death and hell were cast into the lake of fire. This is the second death. And whosoever was not found written in the book of life was cast into the lake of fire.

ROOM 6

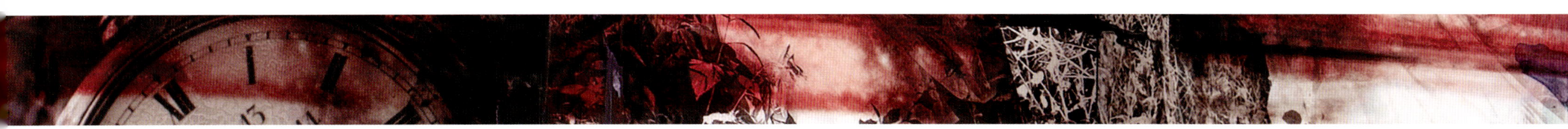

KNOWLEDGE OF THE FUTURE

TRANQUILITY IN THE LIGHT OF TRUTH

IF YOU LOOK CLOSELY AT THE CENTER OF THIS PIECE,
YOU MIGHT SEE THE FIGURE RUNNING TO MEET HER GROOM.

The culmination of the earth, running toward Christ. The bride is invited—to come!

"Let us be glad and rejoice, and give honor to Him: for the marriage of the Lamb is come, and His wife has made herself ready" (Revelation 19:7).

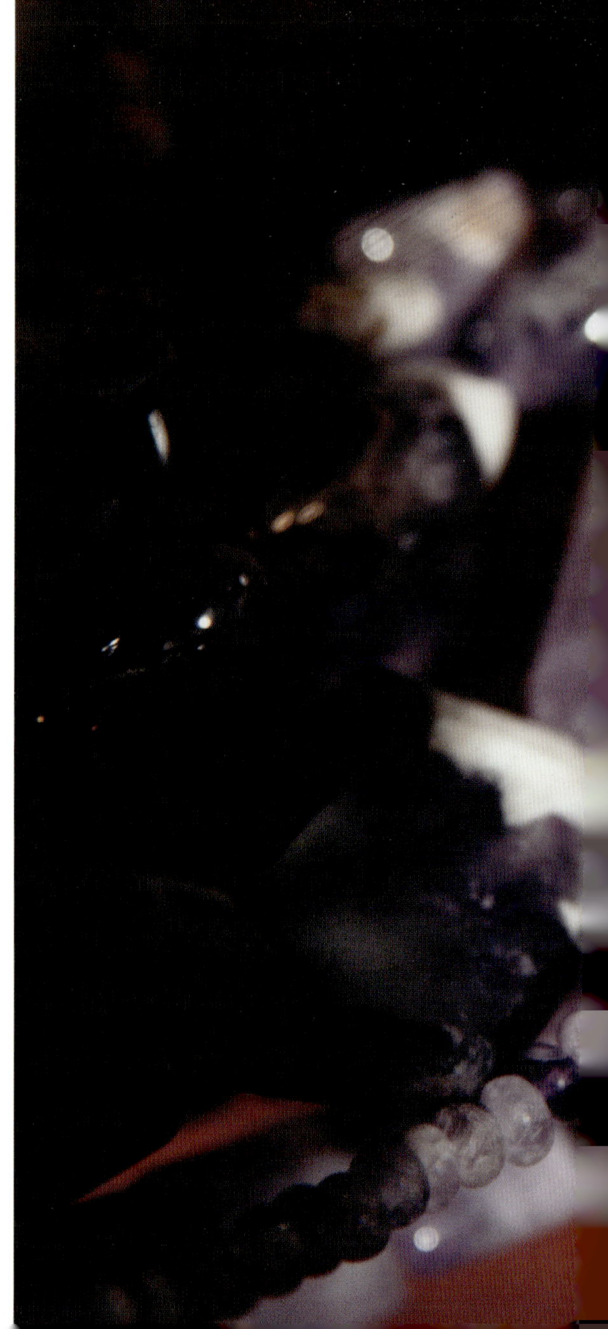

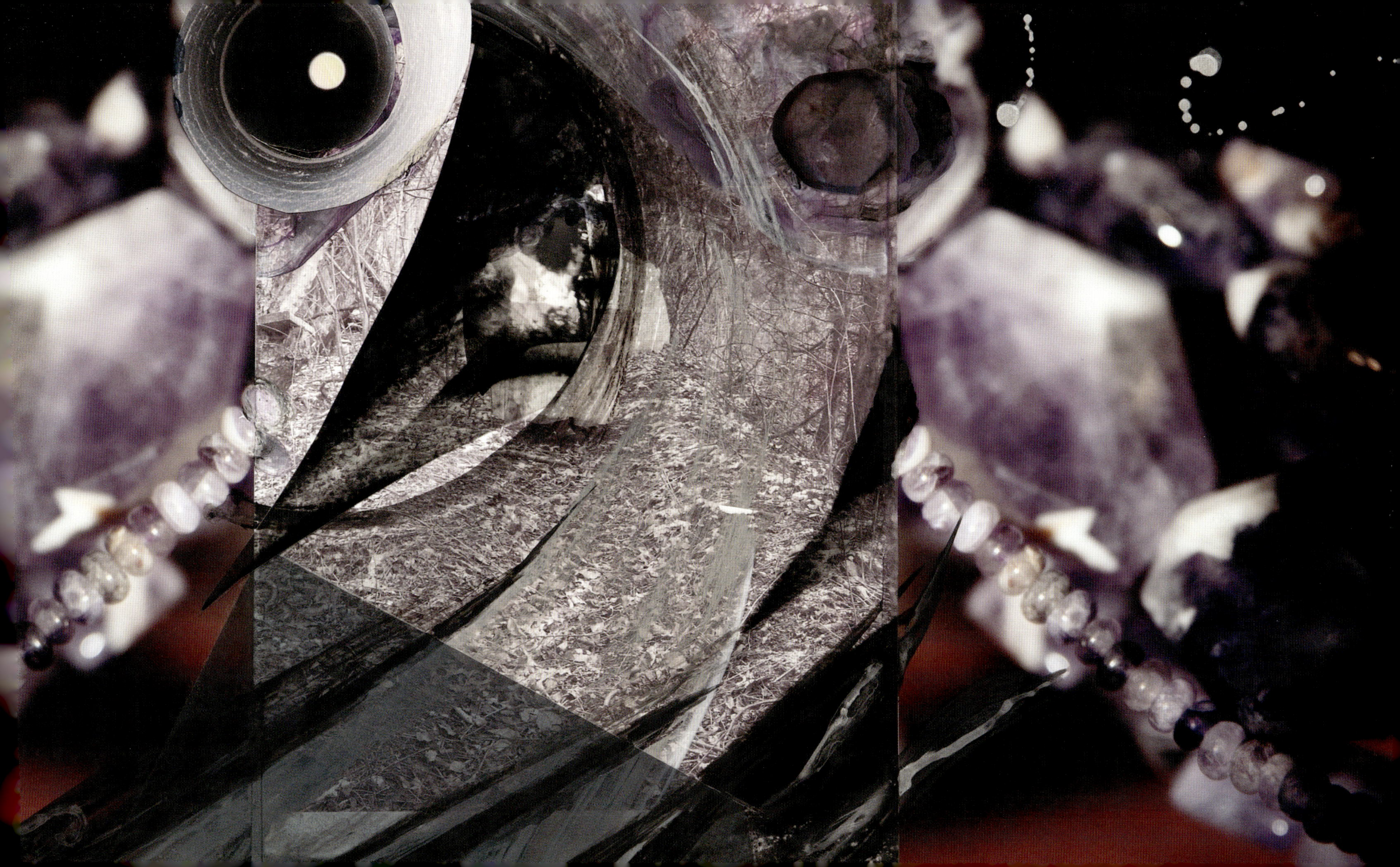

The broken world is coming together. Be certain you're in the right book.

"And I saw the dead, small and great, stand before God; and the books were opened: and another book was opened, which is the book of life" (Revelation 20:12).

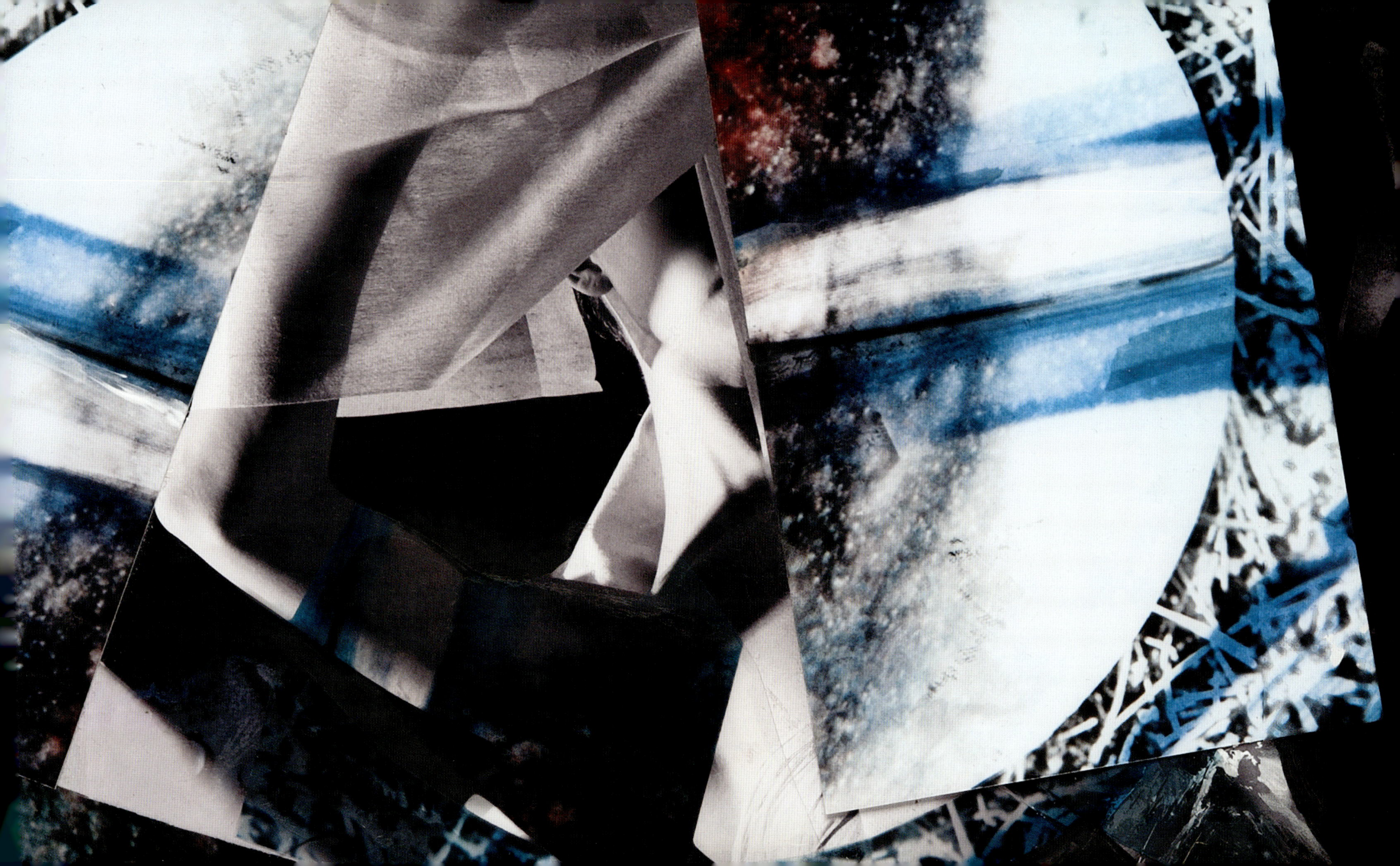

LAKE OF FIRE

The unsealing of God's wrath on the earth.

"And death and hell were cast into the lake of fire.
This is the second death" (Revelation 20:14).

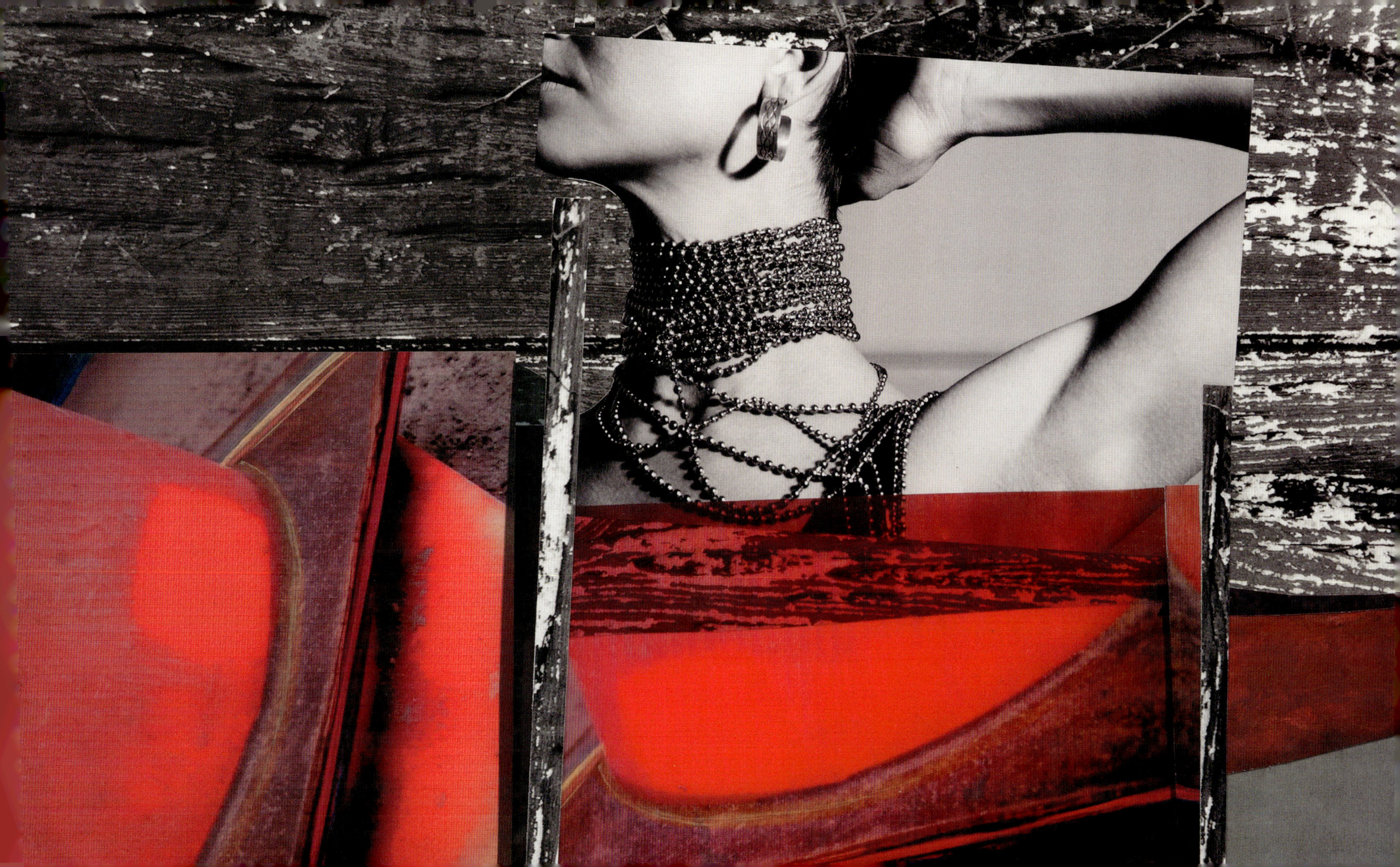

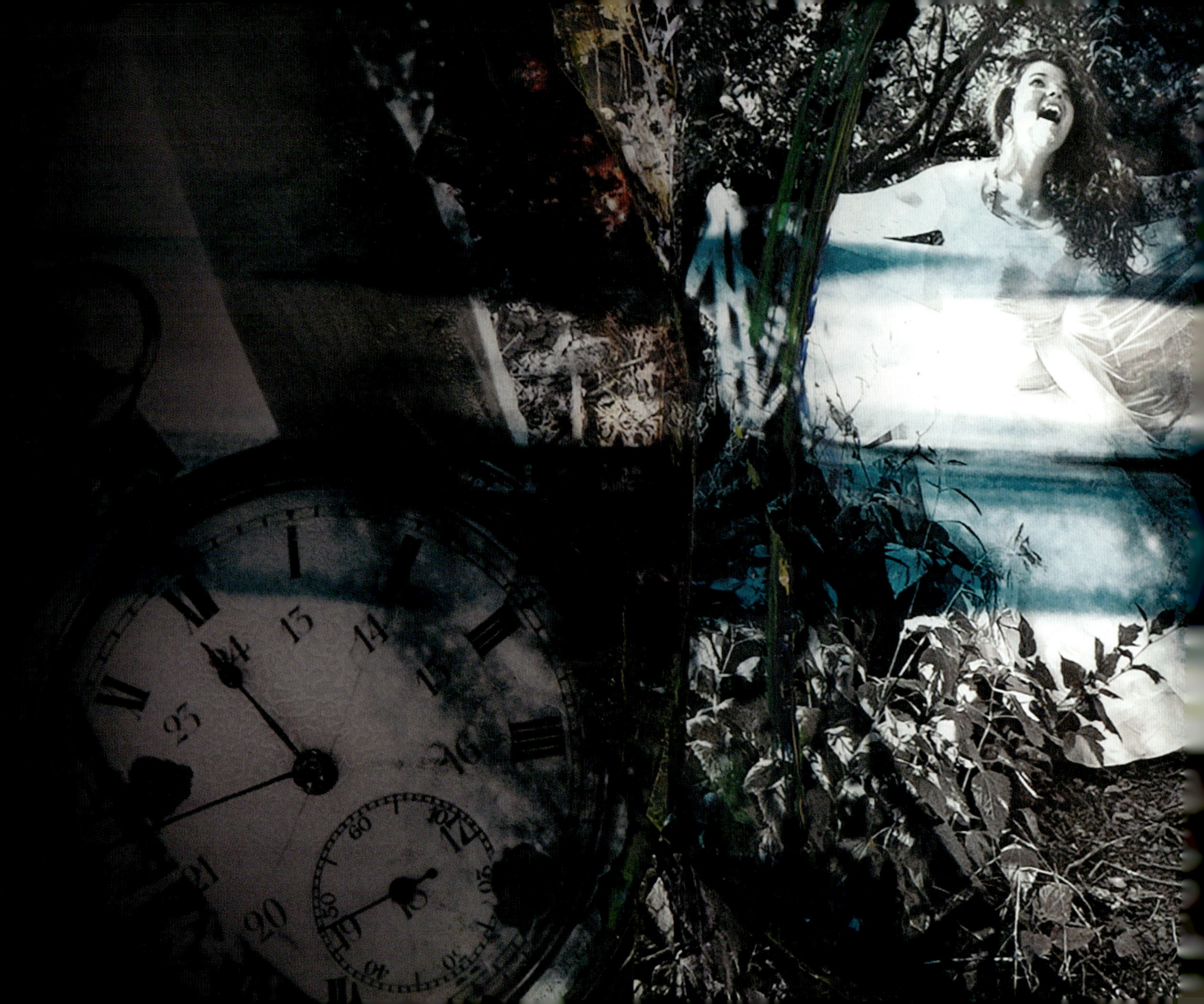

CLOCKWISE

God's timing is always perfect.

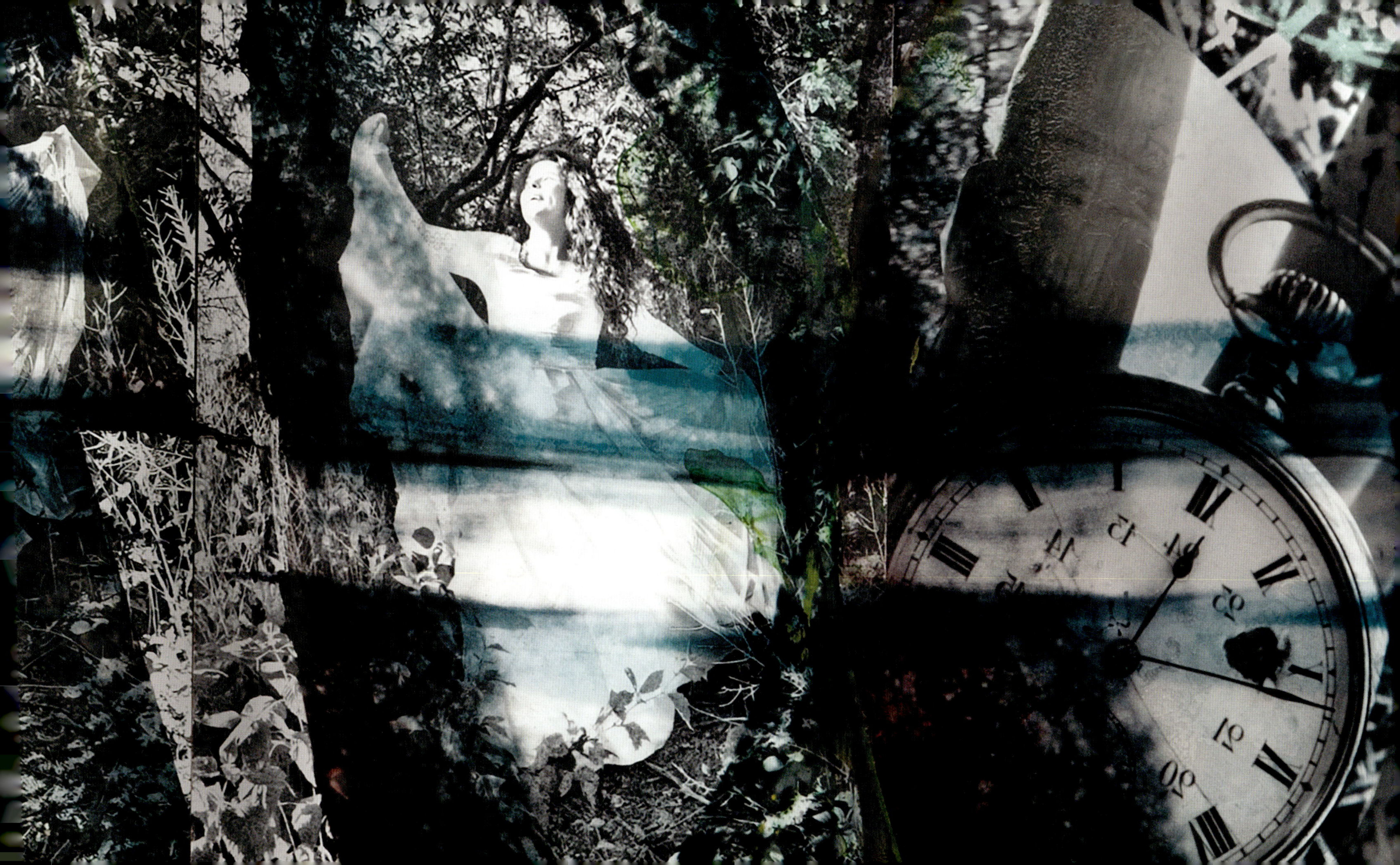

The end of physical life is not the end. We who have hope of an afterlife look forward
to Jesus Christ returning in His resurrection power. We will live in a resurrected body,
a new body, a body like His.

"And again they said, 'Alleluia'" (Revelation 19:3).

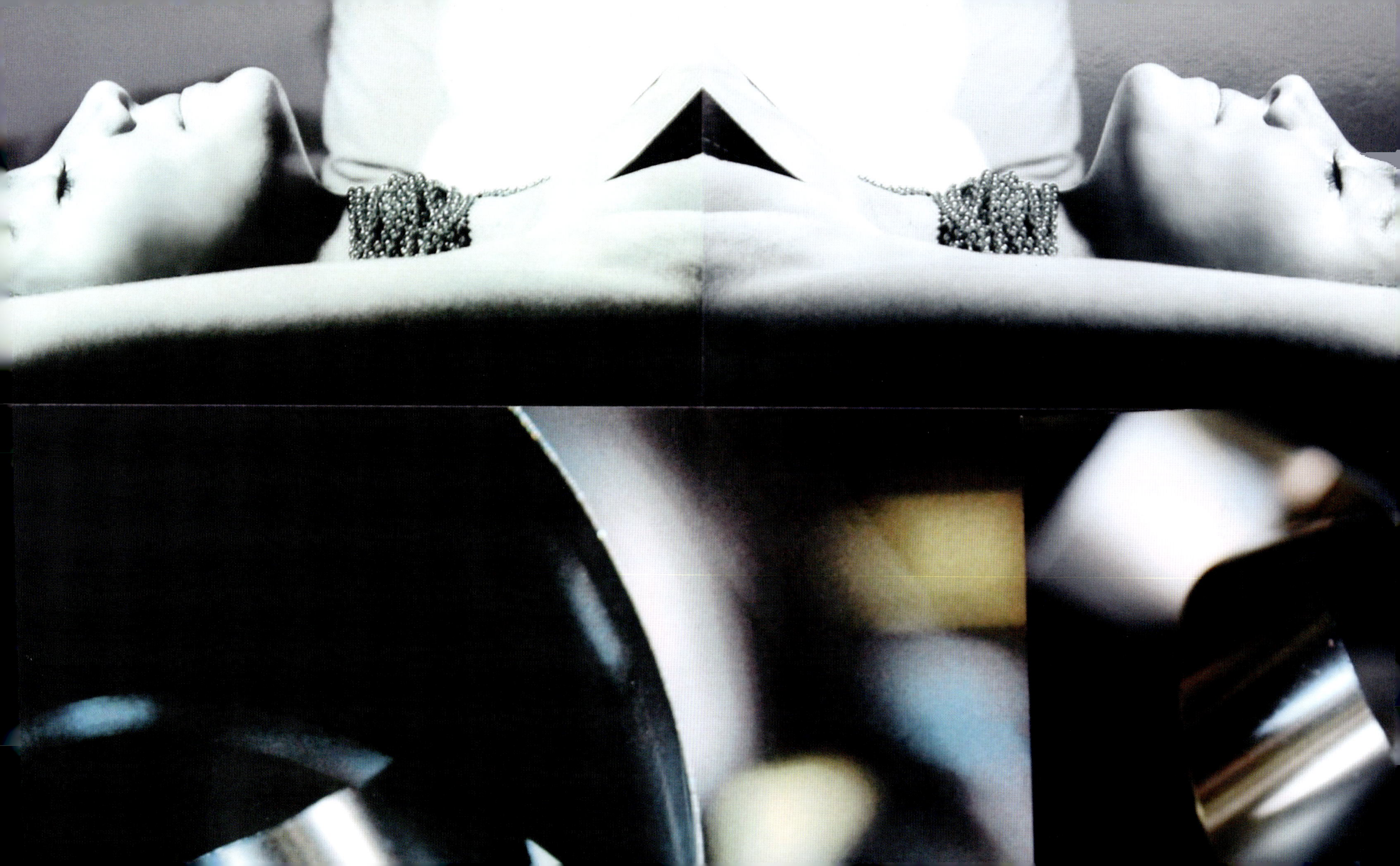

ARISE

Those who are dead in Christ shall arise.
This is the resurrection you don't want to miss!

"Blessed and holy is he that has part in the first resurrection" (Revelation 20:6).

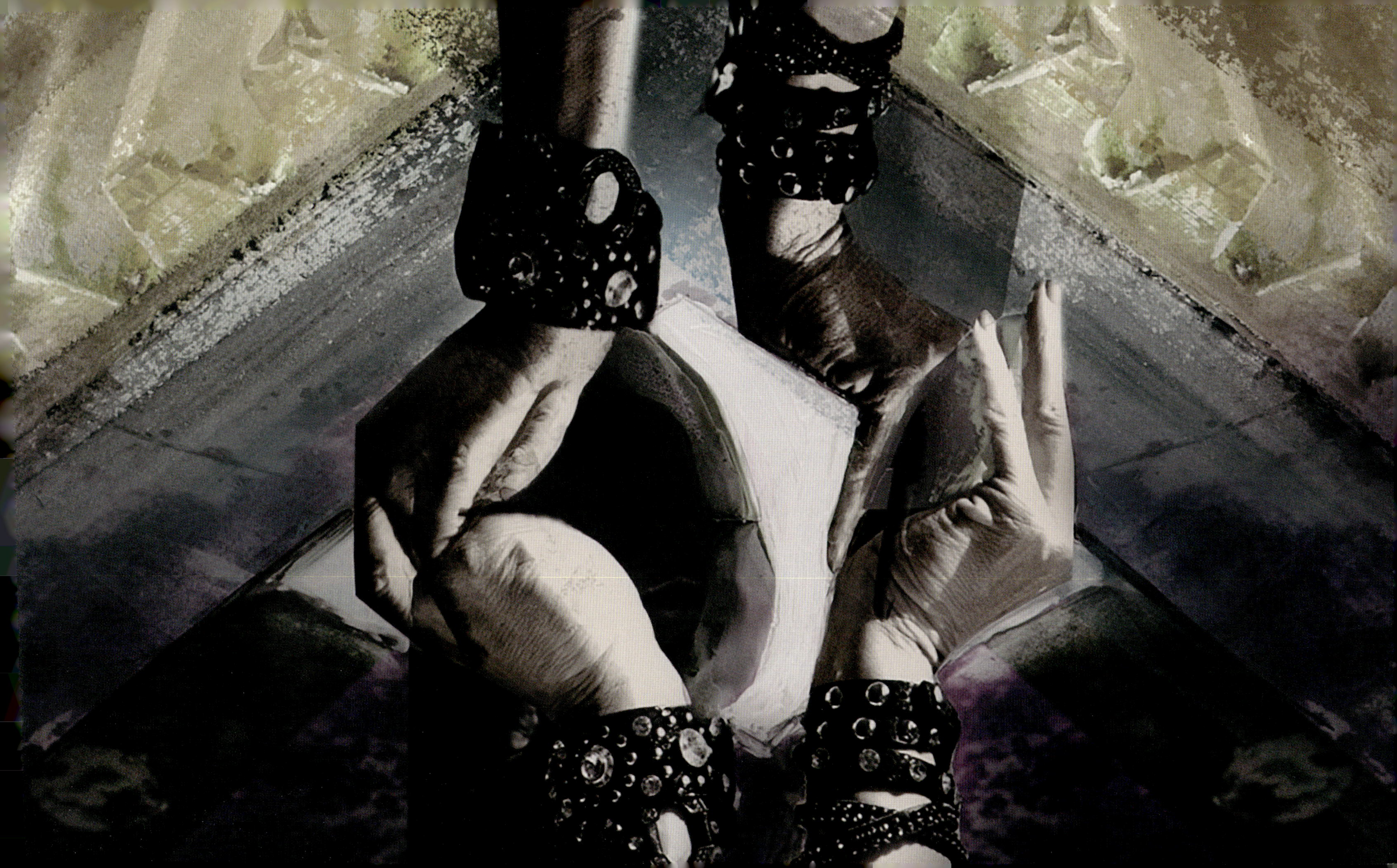

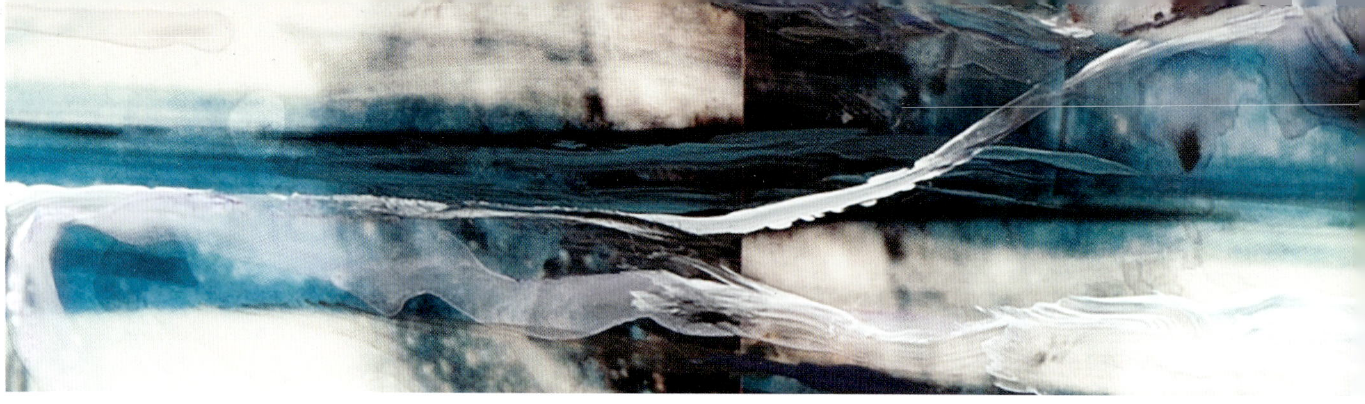

21-22

And I saw a new heaven and a new earth: for the first heaven and the first earth were passed away; and there was no more sea. And I John saw the holy city, new Jerusalem, coming down from God out of heaven, prepared as a bride adorned for her husband.

And I heard a great voice out of heaven saying, Behold, the tabernacle of God is with men, and He will dwell with them, and they shall be His people, and God Himself shall be with them, and be their God. And God shall wipe away all tears from their eyes; and there shall be no more death, neither sorrow, nor crying, neither shall there be any more pain: for the former things are passed away.

And He that sat upon the throne said, Behold, I make all things new. And He said to me, Write: for these words are true and faithful. And He said unto me, It is done. I am Alpha and Omega, the beginning and the end. I will give to him that is thirsty of the fountain of the water of life freely. He that overcomes shall inherit all things; and I will be his God, and he shall be My son. But the fearful, and unbelieving, and the abominable, and murderers, and whoremongers, and sorcerers, and idolaters, and all liars, shall have their part in the lake which burns with fire and brimstone: which is the second death.

And there came me one of the seven angels which had the seven vials full of the seven last plagues, and talked with me, saying, Come here, I will show you the bride, the Lamb's wife. And he carried me away in the Spirit to a great and high mountain, and showed me that great city, the holy Jerusalem, descending out of heaven from God, having the glory of God:

and her light was like to a stone most precious, even like a jasper stone, clear as crystal; and had a wall great and high, and had twelve gates, and at the gates twelve angels, and names written thereon, which are the names of the twelve tribes of the children of Israel: on the east three gates; on the north three gates; on the south three gates; and on the west three gates.

And the wall of the city had twelve foundations, and in them the names of the twelve apostles of the Lamb. And he that talked with me had a golden reed to measure the city, and the gates thereof, and the wall thereof. And the city lies foursquare, and the length is as large as the breadth: and he measured the city with the reed, twelve thousand furlongs. The length and the breadth and the height of it are equal. And he measured the wall thereof, a hundred and forty and four cubits, according to the measure of a man, that is, of the angel.

And the building of the wall of it was of jasper: and the city was pure gold, like to clear glass. And the foundations of the wall of the city were garnished with all manner of precious stones. The first foundation was jasper; the second, sapphire; the third, a chalcedony; the fourth, an emerald; the fifth, sardonyx; the sixth, sardius; the seventh, chrysolyte; the eighth, beryl; the ninth, a topaz; the tenth, a chrysoprasus; the eleventh, a jacinth; the twelfth, an amethyst. And the twelve gates were twelve pearls; every several gate was of one pearl: and the street of the city was pure gold, as it were transparent glass.

And I saw no temple therein: for the Lord God Almighty and the Lamb are the temple of it. And the city had no need of the sun, neither of the moon, to shine in it: for the glory of God did lighten it, and the Lamb is the light thereof. And the nations

of them which are saved shall walk in the light of it: and the kings of the earth do bring their glory and honor into it. And the gates of it shall not be shut at all by day: for there shall be no night there. And they shall bring the glory and honor of the nations into it. And there shall in no wise enter into it any thing that defiles, neither whatsoever works abomination, or makes a lie: but they which are written in the Lamb's book of life.

And he showed me a pure river of water of life, clear as crystal, proceeding out of the throne of God and of the Lamb. In the midst of the street of it, and on either side of the river, was there the tree of life, which bore twelve manner of fruits, and yielded her fruit every month: and the leaves of the tree were for the healing of the nations. And there shall be no more curse: but the throne of God and of the Lamb shall be in it; and his servants shall serve Him: and they shall see His face; and His name shall be in their foreheads.

And there shall be no night there; and they need no candle, neither light of the sun; for the Lord God gives them light: and they shall reign for ever and ever. And he said unto me, These sayings are faithful and true: and the Lord God of the holy prophets sent His angel to show to His servants the things which must shortly be done. Behold, I come quickly: blessed is he that keeps the sayings of the prophecy of this book.

And I John saw these things, and heard them. And when I had heard and seen, I fell down to worship before the feet of the angel which showed me these things. Then says he to me, See you do it not: for I am your fellow-servant, and of your brethren the prophets, and of them which keep the sayings of this book: worship God.

And he says unto me, Seal not the sayings of the prophecy of this book: for the time is at hand. He that is unjust, let him be unjust still: and he which is filthy, let him be filthy still: and he that is righteous, let him be righteous still: and he that is holy, let him be holy still. And, behold, I come quickly; and My reward is with Me, to give every man according as his work shall be. I am Alpha and Omega, the beginning and the end, the First and the Last.

Blessed are they that do His commandments, that they may have right to the tree of life, and may enter in through the gates into the city. For outside are dogs, and sorcerers, and whoremongers, and murderers, and idolaters, and whosoever loves and makes a lie.

I Jesus have sent My angel to testify to you these things in the churches. I am the Root and the Offspring of David, and the Bright and Morning Star.

And the Spirit and the bride say, Come. And let him that hears say, Come. And let him that is thirsty come. And whosoever will, let him take the water of life freely. For I testify to every man that hears the words of the prophecy of this book, If any man shall add to these things, God shall add to him the plagues that are written in this book: and if any man shall take away from the words of the book of this prophecy, God shall take away his part out of the book of life, and out of the holy city, and from the things which are written in this book.

He which testifies these things says, Surely I come quickly. Amen.

Even so, come, Lord Jesus.

The grace of our Lord Jesus Christ be with you all. Amen.

ROOM 7

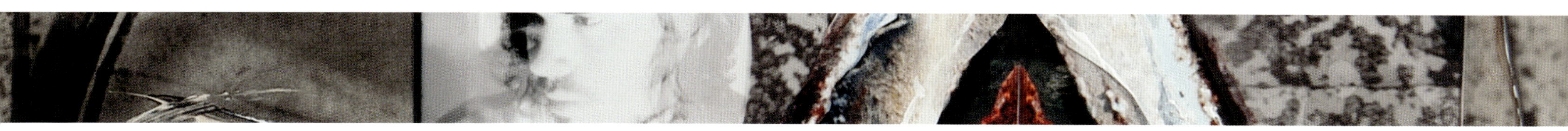

LOOK AT YOUR ETERNAL HOME

This is the end of the end times. Look into the entrance of eternity.

"He will dwell with them, and they shall be His people, and God Himself shall be with them, and be their God. And God shall wipe away all tears from their eyes; and there shall be no more death, neither sorrow, nor crying, neither shall there be any more pain: for the former things are passed away" (Revelation 21:3–4).

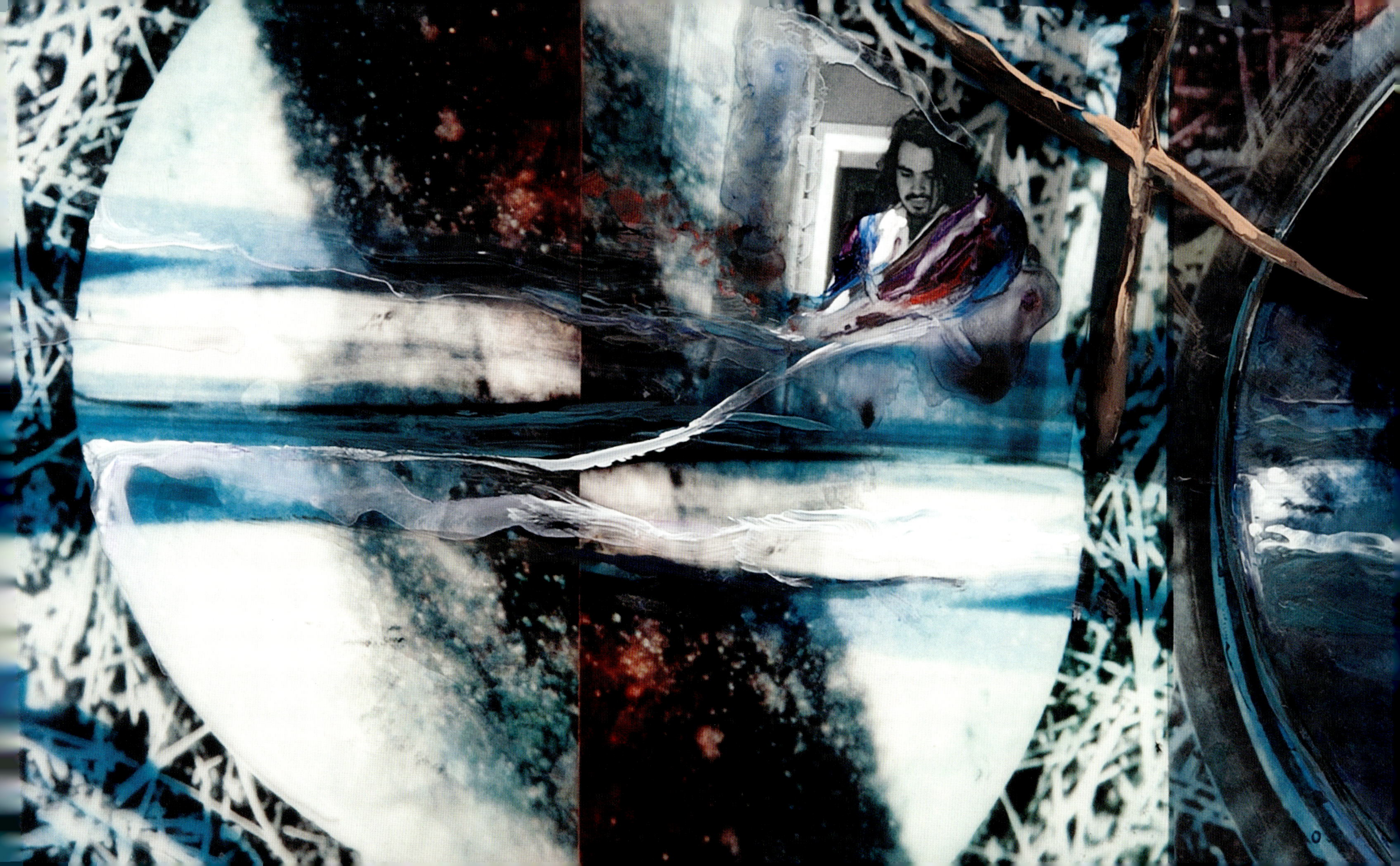

CENTER OF IT ALL

THE JUXTAPOSITION OF THE TWO FOCAL POINTS
DIVIDES OUR ATTENTION BETWEEN THE BRIDE AND GROOM

Love, God's love for us, is the center of it all.

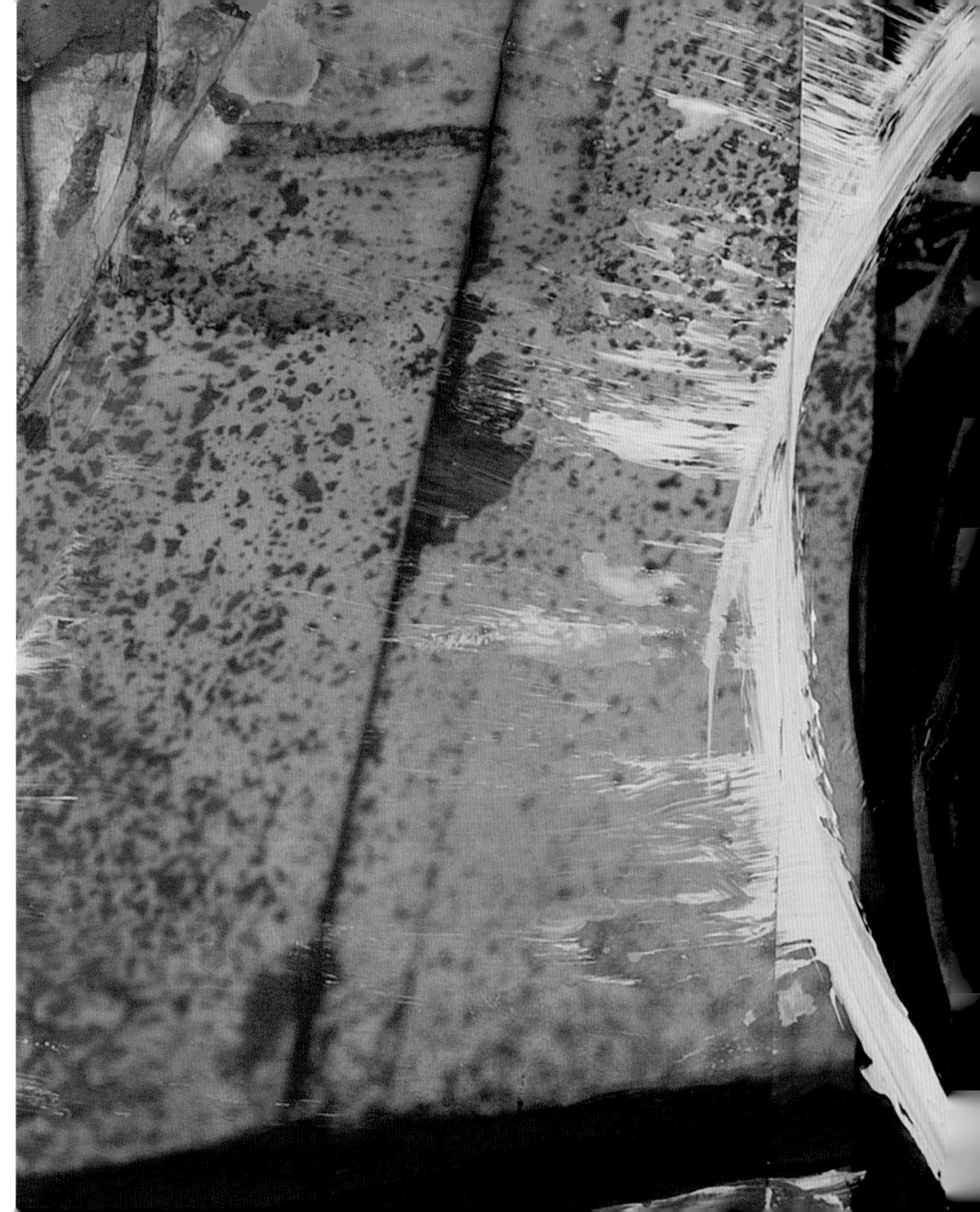

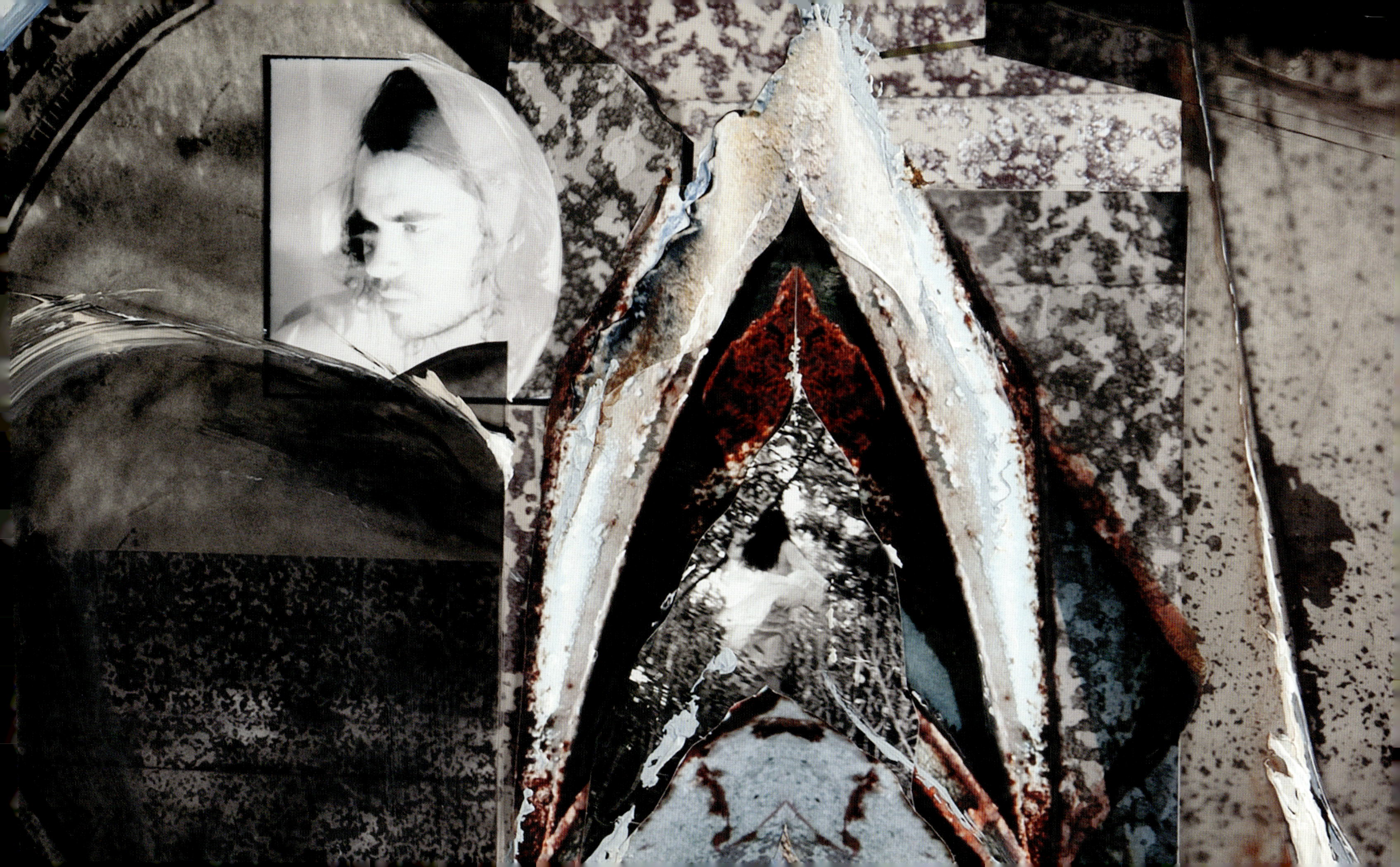

NEW JERUSALEM

TWELVE GATES, TWELVE ANGELS, AND TWELVE MONTHS ARE REPRESENTED IN
THE COLORS SEEN ON THE BORDERS OF THE PIECE. PALE GREEN, PALE GOLD, BLUES,
HONEY, VIOLET, AND YELLOW REPRESENT THE NEW EARTH.

Can you imagine living in the holy city?

*"And he carried me away in the Spirit to a great and high mountain,
and showed me that great city, the holy Jerusalem, descending out
of heaven from God, having the glory of God"* (Revelation 21:10–11).

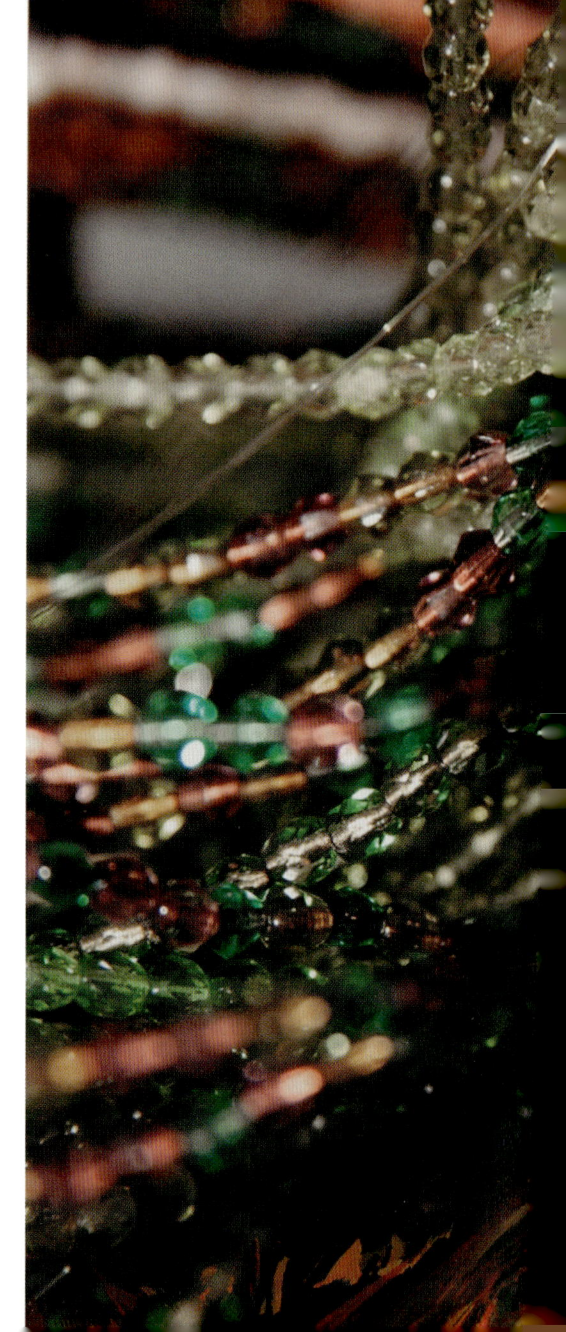

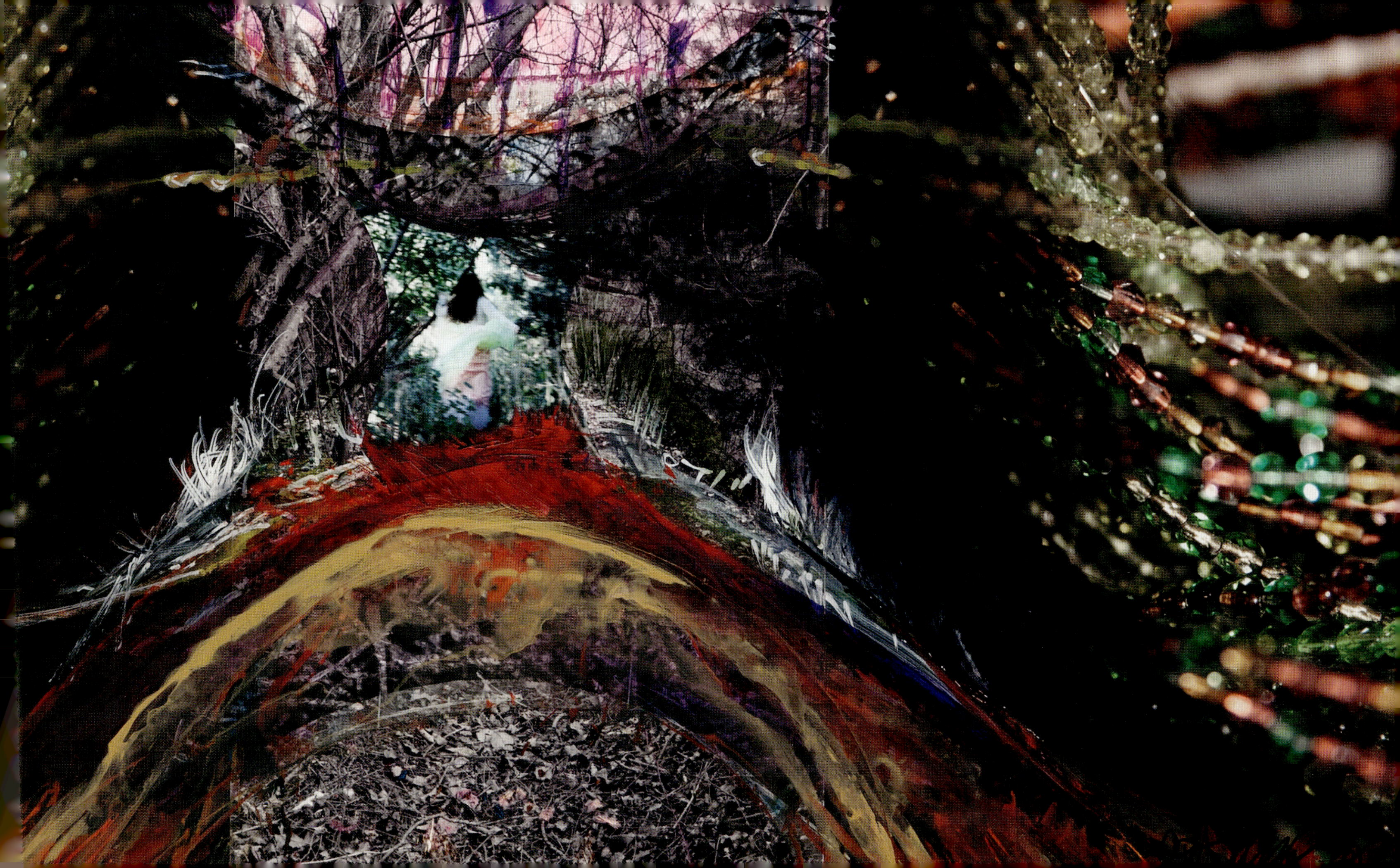

Eternity is established.

"It is done. I am Alpha and Omega" (Revelation 21:6).

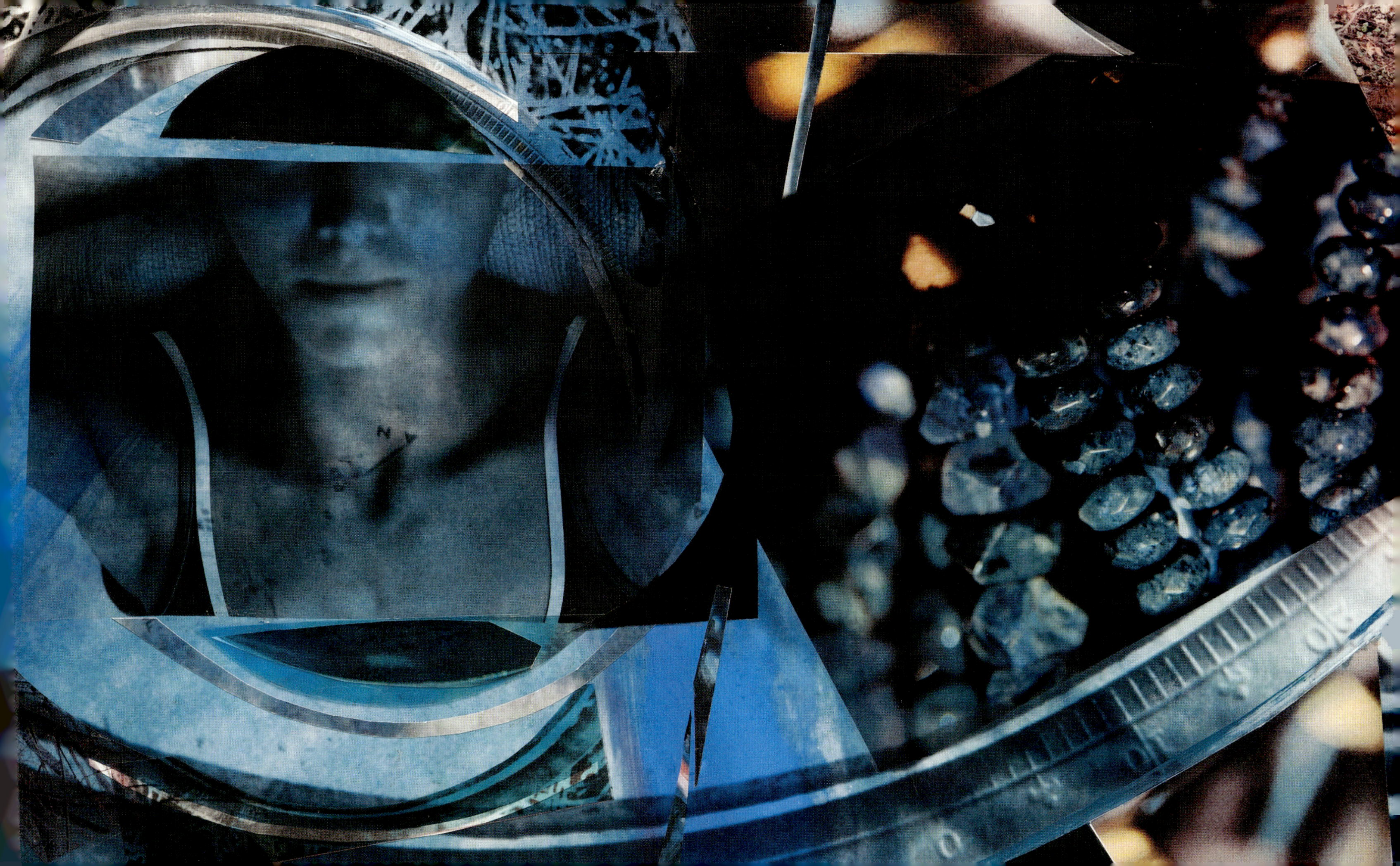

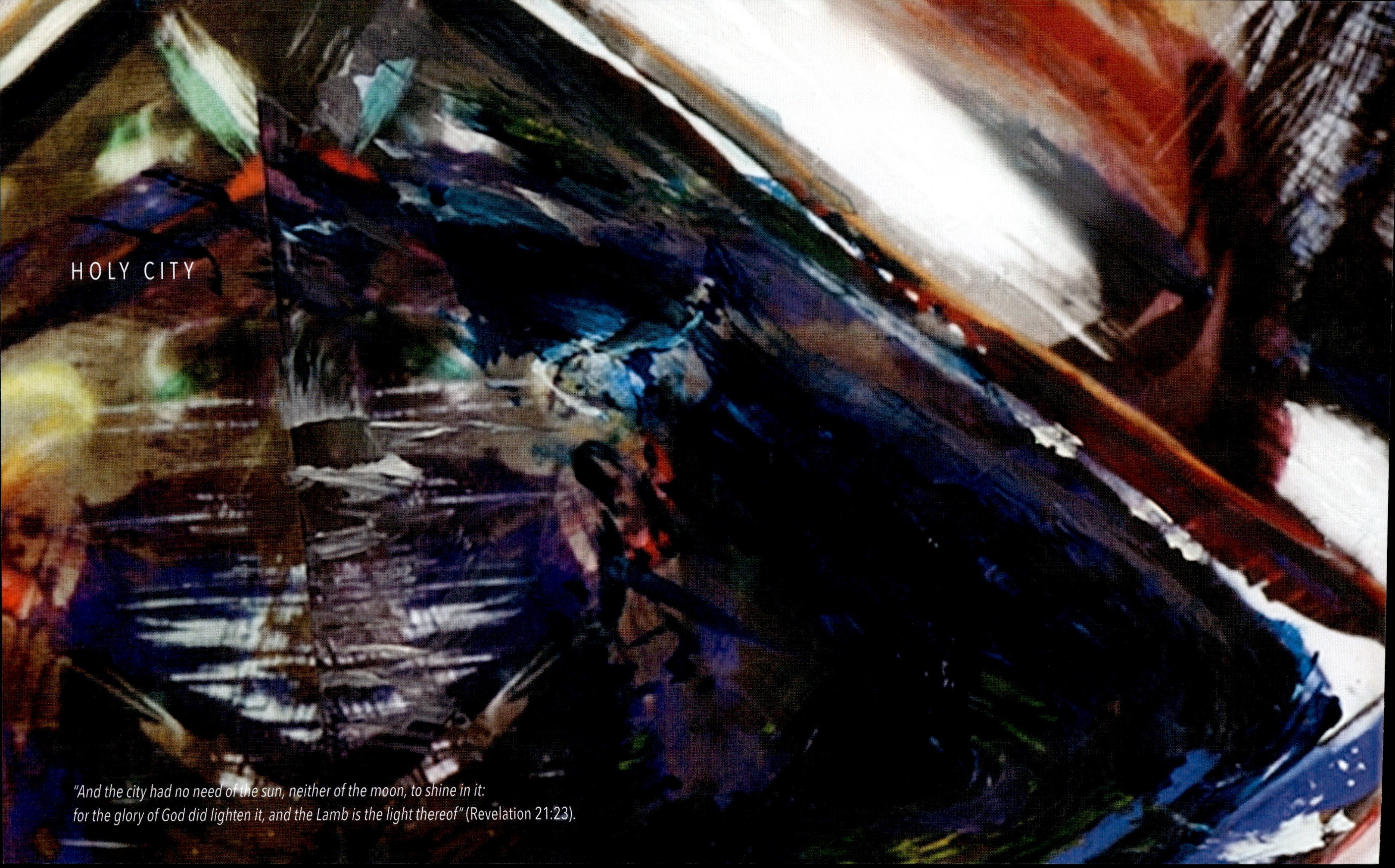

"And the city had no need of the sun, neither of the moon, to shine in it: for the glory of God did lighten it, and the Lamb is the light thereof" (Revelation 21:23).

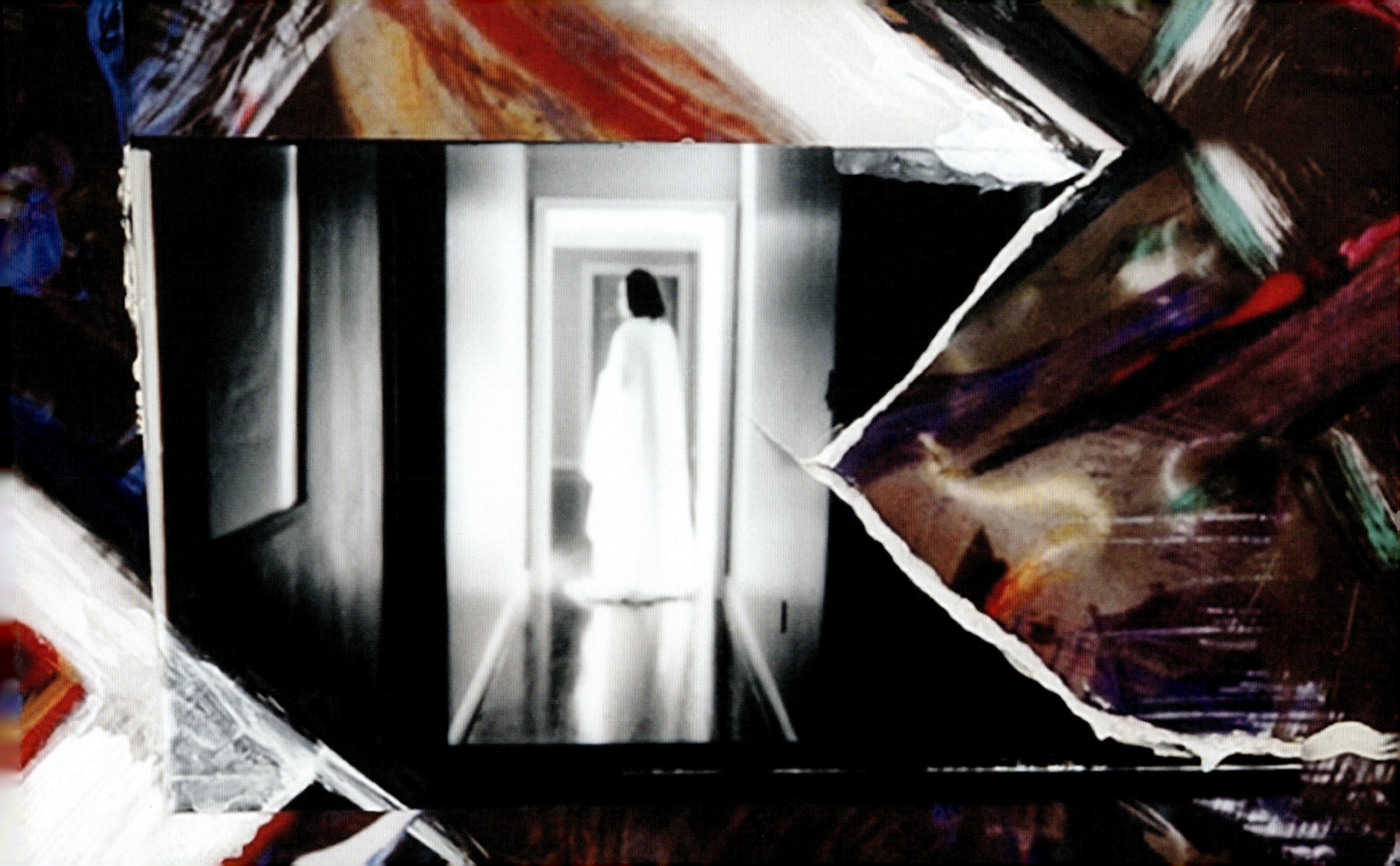

NO MORE CURSE

Open your heart to the invitation!

"And the Spirit and the bride say, Come. And let him that hears say, Come" (Revelation 22:17).

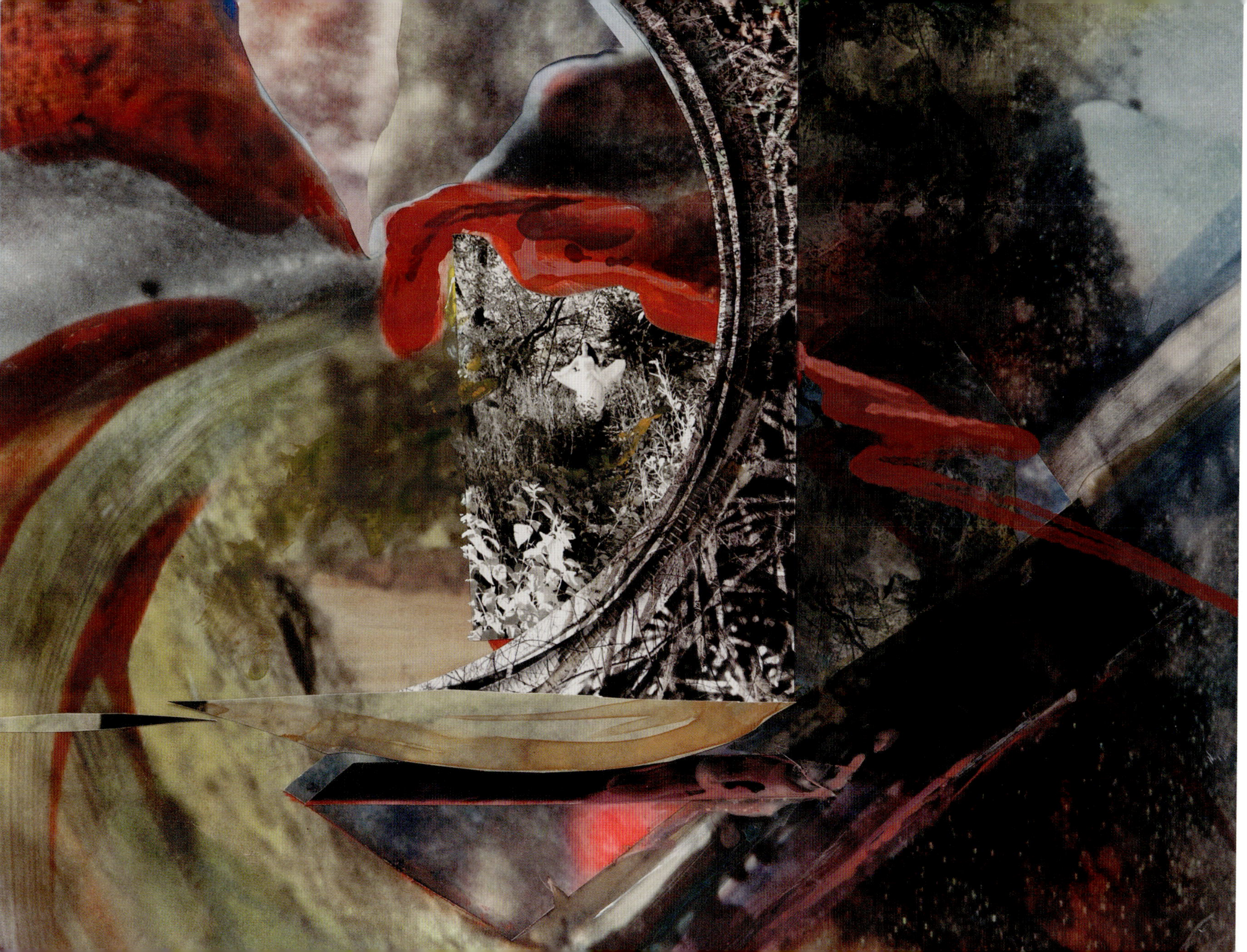

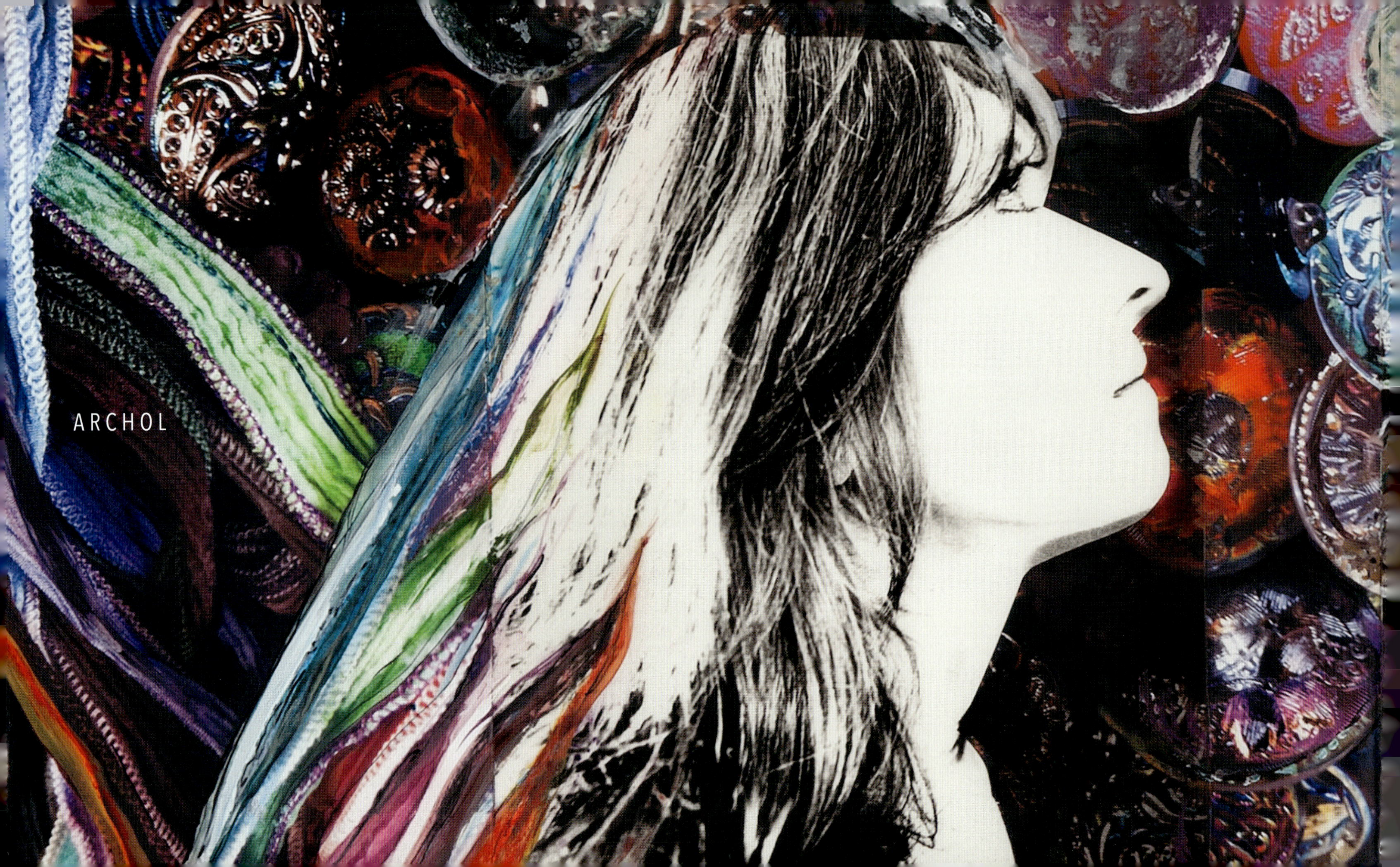
ARCHOL

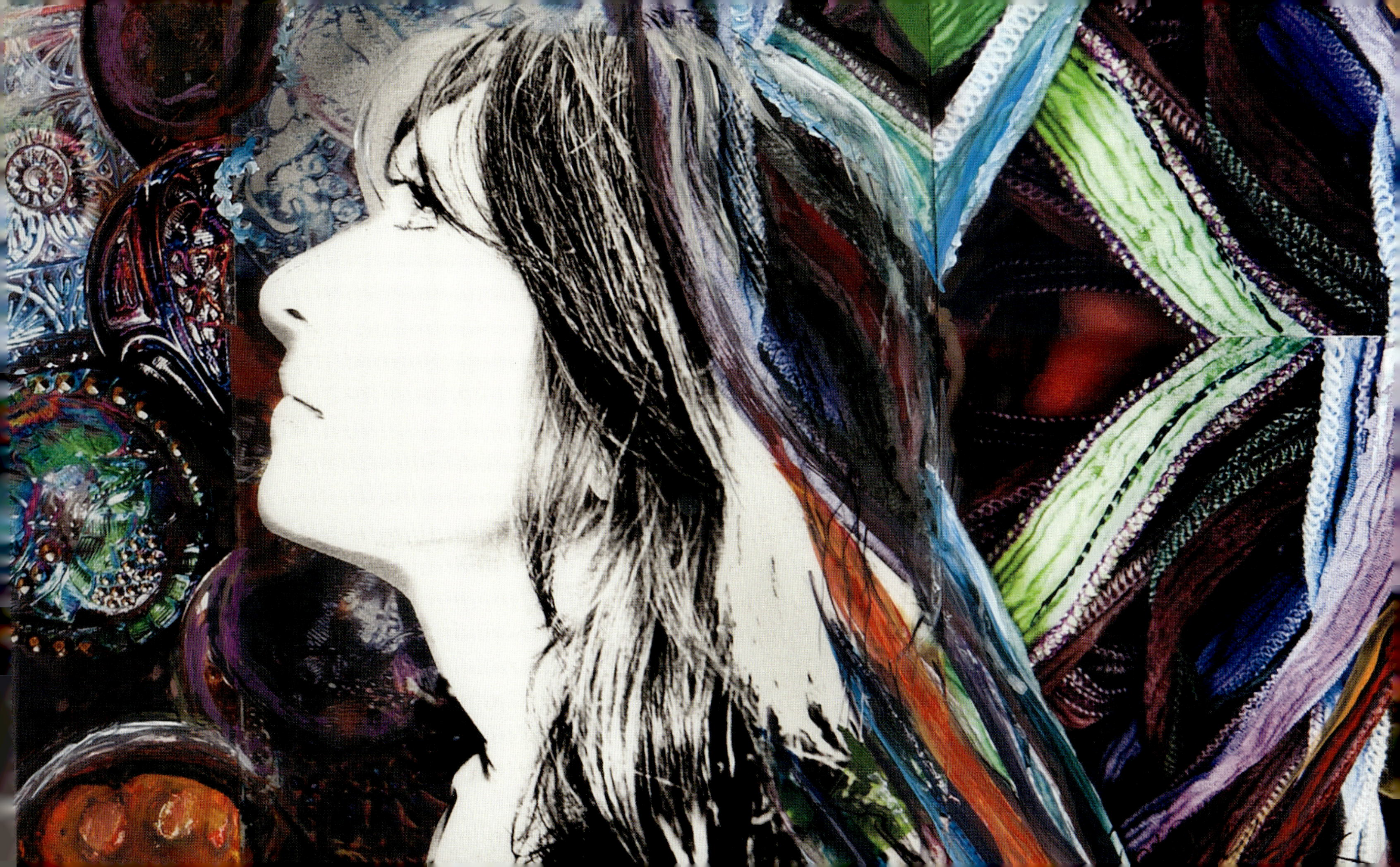

THE INSIDE STORY...

Over twenty years ago, when Marilyn and I both lived in Denver, we would meet twice a week to walk and pray over our country, the nations, and our family needs. Over time, as our friendship grew, I discovered Marilyn's love for the book of Revelation. After reading Revelation and studying Marilyn's *Revelation Encounter* and *The New Millenium & End Time Prophecy Study Guide*, I began getting visions of finished pieces of art. Before long I had over forty images in my head. Inspired, I went into the studio and began organizing what I saw. My creative process of taking photographs, editing them into compositions, and then texturizing and painting over them began to shape into individual pieces of art. Before along, the entire Pittsburgh studio was full of new art. As the project progressed, I shared my heart with Marilyn for bringing clarity and hope to people through the message of love found in the book of Revelation. She guided me when I needed biblical clarity, keeping up with the project as it progressed. On her latest visit to Pittsburgh, she saw the art in its entirety laid out on the studio floor. We began mixing my art with Marilyn's commentary to create a simplified look at the book of Revelation through art. That is how our collaboration began, and I couldn't be more excited about the finished *Revelation Project*.

REVELATIONPROJECT.CO

ABOUT THE AUTHORS

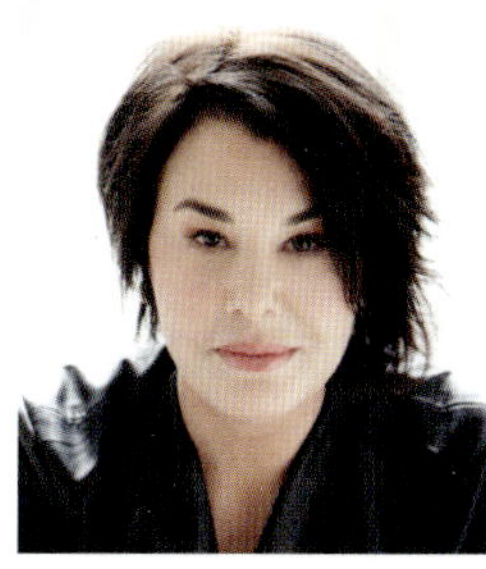

CYNTHIA STANCHAK is a process-based painter who works on unmanipulated photos. A working artist with studios in Pittsburgh and San Francisco, Cynthia has found inspiration from living and working in places such as New York, Illinois, Denmark, Florida, and Colorado. While obtaining a BFA at Drake University in 1979, Cynthia Stanchak blended the realms of photography and painting to create a different kind of art. Over the years, this unique mixed media style attracted a national and international audience of commercial and university galleries, museums and collectors including Canon USA and Pepsi Corporation. She has exhibited her bold, outspoken work at Drake University, Stifle Fine Arts Center/Ogleby Institute, Alternate Gallery, and Pittsburgh Center for the Arts, with features in Artquest.com and ArtSpace.com and lectures at Drake University and Alexandria Museum.

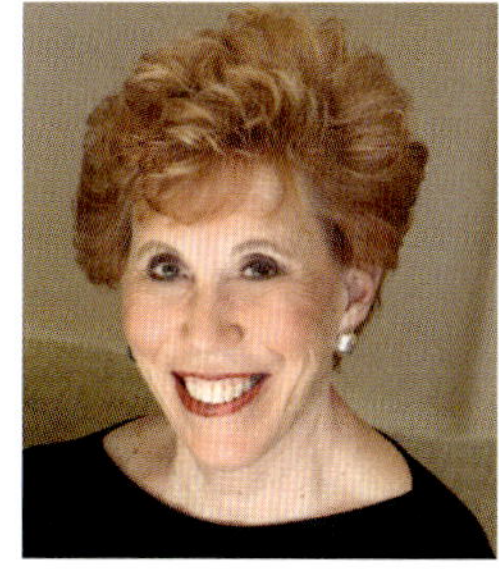

MARILYN HICKEY is founder and president of Marilyn Hickey ministries, a Christian humanitarian organization that has international outreach via television, satellite, books, CDs, DVDs, and crusades. Her previous books with Whitaker House include *Spiritual Warfare*, *Total Healing*, and the 30 Meditations series. She has established an international program of Bible and food distribution and founded a two-year Bible college, Word to the World. Marilyn, along with her late husband, founded the Orchard Road Christian Center in Greenwood Village, Colorado. Marilyn's message of encouragement to all believers is that today can be the best day of your life if Jesus Christ is living in you.

CYNTHIA'S PROCESS

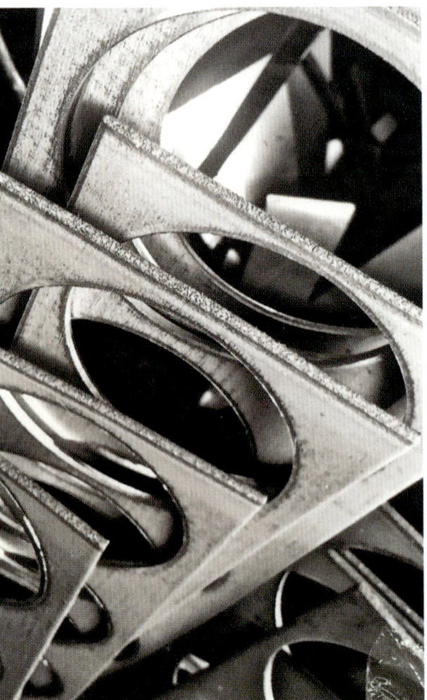

1. The photo

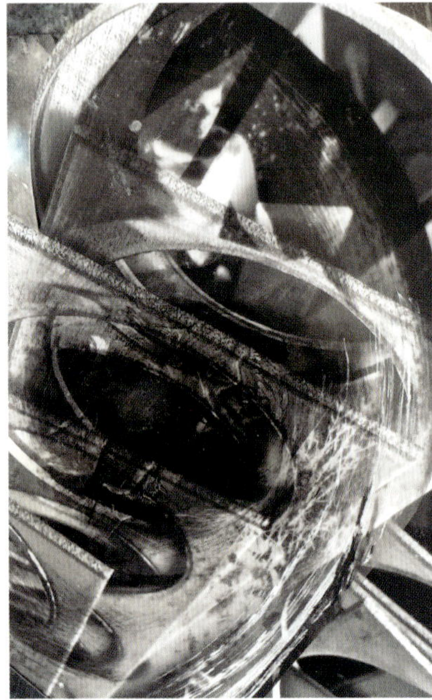

2. Adding layers and texture

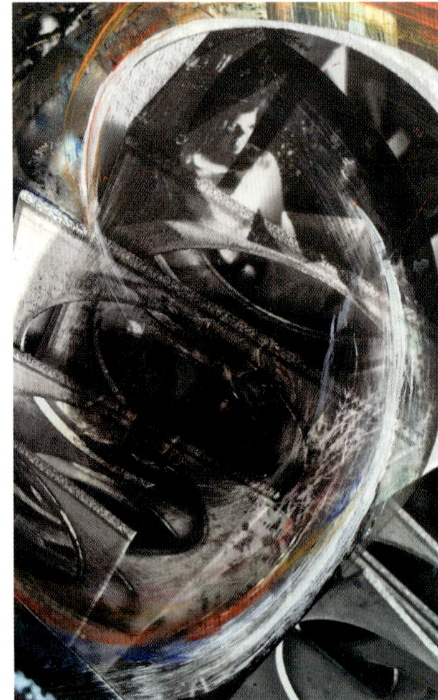

3. Adding color

My work came to life, unexpectedly, one day in the early '80s when I was photographing scrap metal found along the side of the road. Since then, it has evolved along with the cities it has lived in. I combine images that beg to be discovered in their refuse piles with paint and with texture, sometimes overlaying with photographs, and ultimately transforming them into vibrant art. Over the years, the work has changed from 35mm prints to digital representations of lasting forms. The focus of the work, however, is still on the object, unmanipulated in its particular state. Because I am always aware of where an object was originally situated, each piece in the collection is indicative of the place from which the process began, whether conceptually or actually. Considering the eventual context in which the work will find itself, my practice has a heavy design element and is drawn to the qualities of simplicity, minimalism, and functionality often seen in Scandinavian interior design.